THE EXTRAORDINARY BOOK OF SOUTH AFRICAN CRICKET

Kevin McCallum &
David O'Sullivan

PENGUIN BOOKS

PENGUIN BOOKS

Published by the Penguin Group
Penguin Books (South Africa) (Pty) Ltd, 24 Sturdee Avenue, Rosebank, Johannesburg
2196, South Africa
Penguin Group (USA) Inc, 375 Hudson Street, New York, New York 10014, USA
Penguin Group (Canada), 90 Eglinton Avenue East, Suite 700, Toronto, Ontario,
Canada M4P 2Y3 (a division of Pearson Penguin Canada Inc)
Penguin Books Ltd, 80 Strand, London WC2R 0RL, England
Penguin Ireland, 25 St Stephen's Green, Dublin 2, Ireland (a division of Penguin
Books Ltd)
Penguin Group (Australia), 250 Camberwell Road, Camberwell, Victoria 3124,
Australia (a division of Pearson Australia Group Pty Ltd)
Penguin Books India Pvt Ltd, 11 Community Centre, Panchsheel Park, New Delhi –
110 017, India
Penguin Group (NZ), 67 Apollo Drive, Mairangi Bay, Auckland 1310, New Zealand
(a division of Pearson New Zealand Ltd)

Penguin Books (South Africa) (Pty) Ltd, Registered Offices:
24 Sturdee Avenue, Rosebank, Johannesburg 2196, South Africa

www.penguinbooks.co.za

First published by Penguin Books (South Africa))Pty) Ltd 2010

Copyright © David O'Sullivan and Kevin McCallum 2010

ISBN 978 0 143 02667 9

Typeset by Nix Design
Cover design by In The Beginning
Printed and bound by CTP Book Printers, Cape Town

ACKNOWLEDGEMENTS

Kevin McCallum

Between lunch and tea during a Test match, or just after the break in a one-day international, Stuart Hess, the chief cricket writer for *The Star* and Independent Newspapers, and I descend from on high (otherwise called the press box) and take a stroll around the ground. We will buy a beer or two and walk slowly through the crowds, stopping for chats with friends old and new, and soaking up the atmosphere. It's become our tradition, a must-do for each game. Cricket fans are a very different lot, some obsessively marking the match down in their scorebooks, others there for the beer and the girls (and boys), the families with their kids and the corporates wearing ties in the suites.

Then it's back to the press box, where Hess and I are the mickey-takers in chief, breaking up a long day of cricket into fun, bite-sized pieces. This book is dedicated to all those I have spent time with in press boxes, talking cricket. This book is for Peter Robinson, my friend and one of the best cricket writers I have ever read, who was so cruelly taken away from us by cancer a few years ago. This book is to say thank you to Neil Manthorp who always has a smile, a quick line and a good story; to Luke Alfred, who writes superbly; to Ken Borland, who has a mean headbutt on him; to Jane Bramley for the packets of Sparkles, surely the crack cocaine of sweets; to Liam Del Carme, who often accompanies Hess and me on those walks for beer; to Dan Nicholl, who pops around to the press box between flights; and to the commentators and scorers, Pommie, Johnno, Rhino, Jackers, Kepler Wessels, DJ, Keith Lane, Andy Cap, Hussein, Aslam, Zolani and Gerald de Kock, all of whom make a long day zoom past.

I cannot leave out Hans, the caterer at the Wanderers and SuperSport Park; Smiley from Lodge Security; Elize Lombard; Barry Skjoldhammer, a man who loves cricket intensely and is a good mate; Ros Goldin, Nazly Gabier and all at CSA, GCB and Northerns who have been so helpful down the years.

To those former players who always have time for a word, I thank you: to Ali Bacher, who is always just a phone call away and always makes sense; Ekkers, who still owes me a beer; ditto for Charger and not forgetting Shotsy and Adam Bacher. Thanks also to the players, who have entertained me both on and off the field; to Graeme Smith, in my view the greatest captain the country has ever had and a fine Liverpool fan too; to Neil McKenzie, whose knees are holding up just fine and has at least another 10 years of professional cricket left (did I mention that he is also a Liverpool fan?); to Charl Langeveldt, for whom I have been mistaken several times, but I have better hair; to JP, who thinks I drink Hansa morning, noon and night.

A special thanks to all at SAB, who have helped to make this book a success, and to Kate Johns at Standard Bank, who has been a good friend for a long time and hosted the launch as well as buying a chunk of books. To my mother, my two brothers and my surrogate sons, Conor and Breandan, who have finally worked out that their uncle has a 'cool' job. To my friends, with whom I have spent hours at the Grand Slam and the Radium Beer Hall, the best bar in the world. My bosses at *The Star*, sports editor Bafana Shezi and editor Moegsien Williams, and Nazli Thomas at IOL, who have been supportive and allowed me the freedom to scrawl all over their paper and websites.

But, most of all, this book is for Rodney Hartman, taken from us too soon in May 2010. You could not wish for a better man to speak to about cricket; a gentleman who commanded immense respect and who always had a kind word of advice, praise or gentle criticism. This book is dedicated to Rodders. I think he would have liked it.

David O'Sullivan

While writing this book, I found the scorecard of my debut first-class cricket match as a 12-year-old spectator. It was the Boxing Day Currie Cup match between Transvaal and Natal at the Wanderers on 26 December 1974. I remember thinking that Barry Richards was the coolest player on the park, the only one wearing bell-bottomed whites. Well, it was the 1970s. I remember Lee Irvine got a century. I remember a young Clive Rice took some bantering from a couple of drunks, who kept calling him 'Tastic'. I remember he had a full head of hair.

I don't remember the score, but it turns out the match ended in a draw. I also don't remember watching Bob Woolmer as an all-rounder for Natal. Woolmer was one of only four Test players in action in that match, along with Irvine, Richards and Pat Trimborn. Jimmy Cook would become a Test player 18 years later.

But that match was the start of my love of cricket, and my father and I would pack the cooler bag with sarmies, Castle Lager (for him) and Coca-Cola and sit in the south-east stand season after season, watching Transvaal annihilate the opposition. Those were glory days.

Almost 18 years later, on 26 November 1992, the Castles were for me and I was still at the Wanderers, still sitting in the stands, and still watching Jimmy Cook. The match was my first Test as a spectator – South Africa v India. Glory days all over again. The match also ended in a draw.

These days I tend to watch cricket from media boxes or corporate suites, but the thrill of expectation as the first ball of the day is bowled has never left me. The smell of the freshly cut grass, the noise of the crowd, and the crack of a well-struck shot are the same to me today as they were in 1974. I could be a 12-year-old boy with my father all over again. And I still don't care if the match ends in a draw.

Some of the stories in this book I have witnessed as a spectator (the story about South Africa's 5-run win over Australia at the SCG was written purely from memory, so vivid is my recollection of that fantastic day as I sat with my mates in the Bradman Stand). Some of the stories were told to me by former cricketers, and for that Albie During, Ali Bacher, Lawrence Seeff, Clive Eksteen and Steven 'Charger' Jack get a special thanks. Some of the stories I read in the vast collection of cricket books which clutter my study, and for that my dear wife Jacqui gets a special thanks for tolerating the mess. I'm extremely indebted to author, columnist and old Rhodes mate Peter Delmar for his incredible research material. I could have done a simple cut-and-paste of his exhaustive work. Thanks also to Kathleen Heaney for sharing her scrapbook of memories of her husband, the remarkable Tim Heaney, and to Andrew Samson for delving into his encyclopaedic brain and hauling out some vital statistics.

Thanks to David Schröder, the original man-in-charge of this book at Penguin Books, before he decided to seek new adventures abroad. He swears the stress caused by our poor understanding of deadlines had nothing to do with his decision to leave Penguin. Thanks to Reneé Naudé, for designing such a good-looking book, and for taking over as chief whip-cracker. By then, the urgency of deadlines was over so she was spared some grey hairs.

But thanks mainly to the cricketers who have provided me with 36 years of wonderful experiences and great memories. And thanks to my Dad for taking a 12-year-old boy to the Wanderers.

EXTRAORDINARY
INDIVIDUAL
ACHIEVEMENTS

From child prodigy
to Test legend

If one were to write about extraordinary achievements in South African cricket, then the South African cricketer of the century, Graeme Pollock, should be the first story in the book. Of all the players whose performances are recorded in this book, Pollock is probably the only one to whom the adjective 'legendary' is applicable.

Pollock was a child prodigy. As a nine-year-old Port Elizabeth schoolboy, he took all ten wickets and scored 117 – his first century – for Grey Junior School's under-11 side in a match against Union High in Graaff-Reinet. The match was played on a concrete pitch. The young Pollock regularly cleared a six-foot fence on the on-side boundary, hitting the ball into a neighbouring cemetery. He was so keen to get on with the game that he was the first player to go scrambling among the tombstones to retrieve the ball. At 15, he was selected for the South African Schools side. Aged 16 and attending Grey High, he made his first-class debut for Eastern Province, scoring 54 against Border in East London on 9 December 1960.

Just 30 days away from his 17th birthday, he became the youngest South African to score a first-class century – 102 for Eastern Province against Transvaal B at the Wanderers in January 1961.

Three years later, almost to the day, at the age of 19, Pollock scored his first Test century – 122 against Australia in the third Test at the Sydney Cricket Ground in January 1964 – to become the youngest South African Test centurion. The great Don Bradman was so impressed that he told the young Pollock, 'The next time you decide to play like that, send me a telegram.'

Pollock scored 2,256 Test runs in 23 Test matches, with a top score of 274 against Australia in Durban in February 1970. That record stood for 29 years before being broken by Daryll Cullinan, who scored 275 not out against New Zealand in February 1999. That record was equalled by Gary Kirsten (against England in Durban in December 1999), and broken by Graeme Smith (277 against England in Birmingham in July 2003). Appropriately, Cullinan had also broken Pollock's record of being the youngest South African first-class centurion at the same venue where Pollock set the record – Jan Smuts Ground in East London – and in a match featuring the same teams – Border and Eastern Province.

Pollock's Test average is 60.97. Only Bradman has a better Test average for a batsman scoring more than 2,000 Test runs. In 262 first-class matches, Pollock averaged 54.67 – six runs fewer than his Test average.

Pollock scored five Test centuries and two double tons, but his innings of 125 in the second Test against England in Nottingham in August 1965 is rated as his best ever – even by Pollock himself.

South Africa batted first and were in trouble almost immediately, at 16 for 2, when Pollock came to the wicket. He lost three partners before captain Peter van der Merwe joined him at the crease. The pair added 98 for the sixth wicket in just over an hour before Pollock was caught at slip by Colin Cowdrey off Tom Cartwright's bowling.

Pollock was in majestic form, scoring 125 of the 162 runs made in the four partnerships in which he was involved. He faced 145 balls and hit 21 fours. After the lunch break, he hit 91 runs off 90 balls, while Van der Merwe, quite content to prop up one end as Pollock destroyed the England attack, scored just ten runs.

The great cricket commentator Charles Fortune later recalled the knock: 'The power and the artistry of his strokeplay that day [were] awesome. Using his height (six feet, two and a half inches) to full advantage, he drove the English bowling off back foot and front, through the covers, regardless of length. The ball to which other batsmen would have offered a defensive bat was simply struck to the boundary.'

South Africa won the match by 43 runs, to set up an eventual series win against England. The match was a triumph not only for Graeme, but also for his brother, fast bowler Peter Pollock, who took ten wickets in the match (5 for 53 and 5 for 34).

Charles Fortune summed up Pollock's incredible talent: 'If it is permissible to attach the word "genius" to the artistry of a batsman, then Graeme Pollock is such among cricketers. Like others so acknowledged, he was ever the master craftsman. Perhaps the all-important factor was that from the start, the bowling he faced was more skilled and demanding than will have come the way of many others.'

Barry Richards – one of the greats

South African cricket is peppered with extraordinary moments, and many are provided by the great players of the day. Barry Richards is one such player, and although he played only four Test matches, he made his mark plying his trade in provincial cricket in South Africa, Sheffield Shield cricket in Australia and county cricket in England, playing for Natal, South Australia and Hampshire.

One of his most memorable knocks came in a Sheffield Shield match against Western Australia at the WACA in Perth on 20 November 1970, when he scored an incredible 356 runs in one day. He hit 48 fours and a six in that knock, which lasted six hours and 12 minutes. And it wasn't as if he was facing some journeymen bowlers in the Western Australia side. He was up against Australian Test bowlers Garth McKenzie, Dennis Lillee, John Inverarity and Tony Mann, and England spin bowler Tony Lock.

South Australia won the match by an innings and 111 runs. That season, Richards scored 1,538 for his team, at a average of 109.86, including scores of 224, 356, 146, 155, 178 and 105.

A long-standing record broken - not for long

Boland's Terence Lazard broke a South African batting record that had stood for over 54 years, only to hold the landmark for a mere three weeks. In September 1993, Lazard scored 307 not out for Boland against Western Province at Worcester, breaking a record that had been set in December 1939 by Eric Rowan for the highest individual score in a first-class cricket match. Rowan had scored 306 not out for Transvaal against Natal in Johannesburg.

But instead of Lazard's record taking a further 50-odd years to beat, Daryll Cullinan broke the record just three weeks after it had been officially ratified. Cullinan scored 337 not out for Transvaal against Northern Transvaal in Johannesburg in October 1993 in an innings lasting four minutes short of 11 hours, off 528 balls and including 41 fours and three sixes. Cullinan's record has since been broken by Stephen Cook, son of Jimmy Cook. Playing for the Highveld Lions, he scored 390 against the Warriors in a SuperSport series match in East London in October 2009. His knock took 14 hours and included 53 boundaries and one six. Cook's father Jimmy had played with Cullinan in the match in which he scored his 337.

Peter Kirsten's six tons in seven knocks

In the New Year's match between Western Province and Transvaal in January 1977, a young Peter Kirsten achieved the remarkable feat of having scored six first-class centuries in seven innings. Only three other batsmen had managed such a record (Ernest Tyldesley, Vijay Merchant and Wally Hammond), and only three others had gone better, scoring six out of six (CB Fry, Don Bradman and Mike Procter). Playing for Western Province, Kirsten knocked up 173 not out and 103 against Eastern Province at Newlands in December 1976 – at the age of 21 the youngest South African to reach the milestone of a century in each innings of a first-class match.

He scored his next first-class ton – 107 – for South African Universities against Orange Free State, and followed that with 165 for Western Province against Transvaal at the Wanderers. In the second innings, Kirsten was dismissed for 22, but returned to century-making form against Natal at Kingsmead with a knock of 111.

A capacity crowd came to Newlands to watch him score 128 against Transvaal. Fans charged onto the field to congratulate him as he reached his century, with fellow batsman, Hylton Ackerman, flamboyantly bowing down before the young maestro. Kirsten topped the batting rankings for the 1976/77 season with 1,074.

Mike Procter equalled the record jointly held by the legendary CB Fry and Don Bradman of six tons in six innings while coaching and playing for Rhodesia in the Currie Cup in 1970/71. He started with 119 against Natal B and 129 against Transvaal B at Salisbury in November 1970. In Bloemfontein against Orange Free State, he scored 107 in just over an hour, and followed that with 174 against North-Eastern Transvaal in Pretoria and 106 against Griquas in Kimberley. With the eyes of the cricket world on him, he equalled the Fry/Bradman record with a sixth successive century and his highest score of the six-innings run – 254 against Western Province in Salisbury in March 1971. In the final match of the season, between Transvaal and a Rest of South Africa XI, Procter's remarkable run came to an end when he was out hit wicket for 22.

Barlow's five-ball blitz

Eddie Barlow produced an extraordinary spell of bowling in an unofficial Test match between the Rest of the World and England at Headingley in July/August 1970. The match's unofficial status was the result of the South African tour of England in 1970 being cancelled owing to political pressure from the anti-apartheid movement. The Test and County Cricket Board organised five unofficial Tests, and selected a powerful Rest of the World XI to take on England. Garry Sobers captained the side, which included fellow West Indians Clive Lloyd, Rohan Kanhai, Lance Gibbs and Deryck Murray. Five South Africans were included – Barry Richards, Eddie Barlow, Graeme and Peter Pollock and Mike Procter. Two Pakistanis, Intikhab Alam and Mushtaq Mohammad, and Australia's Graham McKenzie made up the rest of the powerful squad.

In the fourth match of the series in Leeds, Barlow took a hat-trick in England's first innings. After a dot ball, he got a fourth wicket in five balls. First he bowled Alan Knott and Chris Old. The hat-trick wicket was unusual. Don Wilson got a big nick onto his pad and the ball skied to silly point where the catch was easily taken by an opposition player – England's 12th man, Mike Denness. The Rest of the World XI was short of two players through injury – Barry Richards and Rohan Kanhai – but had only one substitute, so Denness was asked to field for the opponents. He took the catch, but was too embarrassed to appeal. He later said his teammates didn't hold it against him.

Barlow then got the wicket of Ray Illingworth two balls later to finish a remarkable over. Barlow took 7 for 64 in the innings, and had match figures of 12 for 142 as the Rest of the World won by two wickets.

White Lightning's first strike

Allan Donald is in a group of just four other bowlers to have taken five wickets on debut in a one-day international match. In South Africa's first official one-day international against India at Eden Gardens in Calcutta on 10 December 1991, Donald – who would later be nicknamed White Lightning – took 5 for 29 in 8.4 overs as India beat South Africa by three wickets. His first victim was the great Ravi Shastri, caught by Dave Richardson off Donald's fifth ball in ODI cricket for a duck. Ten South Africans made their debut that day: Jimmy Cook, Andrew Hudson, Peter Kirsten, Adrian Kuiper, Clive Rice (captain), Richard Snell, Brian McMillan, Richardson, Tim Shaw and Donald. Only Kepler Wessels had played ODI cricket before – 54 matches for Australia.

The West Indian Fidel Edwards holds the record for the most wickets taken on debut in an ODI when he took 6 for 22 against Zimbabwe in Harare in November 2003. The next most successful South African ODI debutant bowlers are Vernon Philander (4 for 12 against Ireland in Belfast); Shaun Pollock (4 for 34 against England in Cape Town); Dave Rundle (4 for 42 against Australia in Brisbane); and Lonwabo Tsotsobe (4 for 50 against Australia in Perth).

Swashbuckling Klusener

The big-hitting Lance Klusener enjoyed an extraordinary run of form with the bat in 1999, when he broke the record for runs scored in one-day internationals between dismissals. Klusener scored a remarkable 400 runs between dismissals, starting with a one-day series against New Zealand. He began with an unbeaten knock of 103 in Auckland in February 1999, and racked up further scores of 35 not out, 13 not out and 35 not out in that series. In the 1999 World Cup in England, where he was named Man of the Tournament, he made 12 not out, 52 not out, 48 not out, 52 not out and 46 not out, before being dismissed for 4. The record has since been broken by Mohammad Yousuf of Pakistan with his 405 ODI runs between dismissals.

Five Test tons in a row

Jacques Kallis is in a group of only three batsmen to score hundreds in five successive Tests. Kallis's remarkable run began in the first Test against the West Indies in Johannesburg in December 2003, when he got 158 in the first innings. In the second Test in Durban, Kallis scored 177 in the first innings, followed by a second-innings knock of 130 not out in the third Test in Cape Town and another innings of 130 not out in the first innings of the fourth Test in Centurion. Kallis took his purple patch to New Zealand two months later, where he achieved the rare feat of five tons in five Tests with a second-innings score of 150 not out in Hamilton in the first Test.

He fell just 29 runs short of a remarkable six tons in six Tests in the second Test in Auckland. The other two batsmen in this unique club are India's Gautam Gambhir and Pakistan's Mohammed Yousuf. Don Bradman went one better, scoring three figures in six consecutive Tests – all against England.

A hat-trick start

The most extraordinary start to a one-day international occurred at the City Oval in Pietermaritzburg on 14 February 2003. The Oval was hosting its first ever international cricket match, a World Cup clash between Sri Lanka and Bangladesh. Sri Lankan fast bowler Chaminda Vaas ensured it would go down in the history books by taking a hat-trick with the first three balls of the match. He bowled Hannan Sarkar, then caught and bowled Mohammad Ashraful, before claiming the wicket of Ehsanul Haque for the hat-trick. It's the first time the first three balls of an international have resulted in wickets. Vaas conceded four runs off his fourth ball, and then trapped Sanwar Hossein LBW for a fourth wicket in that dramatic opening over. Sri Lanka won the match by ten wickets, and Vaas's 5 for 25 earned him the privilege of planting a tree at the ground – an honour bestowed on players who score a century or take five wickets at the City Oval.

The Oval is unusual in that it is a first-class cricket ground which has a tree within the boundary.

A fielder flies into history

In his first 28 ODI matches, Jonty Rhodes had taken just nine catches, though his fielding exploits had prevented the opposition from scoring bucketfuls of runs. However, saved runs are never credited in the official scorecard, and as the cricketing cliché goes, catches win matches. In a sport in which wicketkeepers may often take three or four catches per match, it's a little unusual for an outfielder to take more than three catches. So when Rhodes took five catches in a single ODI, it was a jaw-dropping achievement.

The match in question was a Hero Cup game against the West Indies at the Brabourne Stadium, in what was then called Bombay, on 14 November 1993. South Africa were defending a meagre 170 for 5 in 40 overs, with Rhodes having scored 40 at almost a run a ball.

That might not have been a match-winning performance, but his fielding exploits were. Rhodes first got rid of Brian Lara, who had prodded a ball a few metres towards square leg. Rhodes charged in from backward point and launched himself at the ball, sliding up on his stomach towards the disbelieving Lara with the ball firmly in his grasp.

Phil Simmons was next to go, courtesy of a one-handed catch as Rhodes dived to snatch the ball at short mid-wicket. Jimmy Adams was then gleefully snaffled up at mid-wicket.

The fourth catch was the pick of the bunch. Anderson Cummins cut a ball from Allan Donald, which flew down towards third man. Rhodes threw himself into the air, his right hand stretched out high and behind his body, to take a spectacular catch.

Opener Desmond Haynes had retired hurt earlier in the innings, but had to return at the end of the innings in a vain bid to win the match. He ended up lobbing a routine catch to Rhodes to give him the world record of five in an ODI, and South Africa won the match by 41 runs.

Rhodes's incredible abilities in the field first achieved international prominence during the 1992 World Cup. In South Africa's astounding victory against Australia at the Sydney Cricket Ground on 26 February 1992, Rhodes, making his international debut, had run out Craig McDermott, demonstrating that he was not to be trifled with in the field.

The moment that created Rhodes as a fielding phenomenon came four games later during the World Cup match against Pakistan in Brisbane on 8 March 1992. Pakistan were chasing a rain-reduced target of 194 in 36 overs, with Inzamam-ul-Haq and Imran Khan putting on 85 for the third wicket as Pakistan reached 135 for 3. The run chase was on, with Pakistan needing almost nine runs an over.

Inzamam, a notoriously slow runner given his bulk, was hit on the pad by a ball from Brian McMillan and he attempted to burgle a quick single. Imran saw Rhodes swooping on the ball, and – perhaps remembering McDermott's fate earlier in the tournament – sent Inzamam back. Inzamam turned like a battleship in a blizzard, and tried to get back to the safety of his crease.

Rhodes dashed in from his customary cover-point position, gathered the ball in full stride and opted to sprint for the wicket rather than risk the throw. As the lumbering Inzamam battled to make his ground, Rhodes made sure of his victim's fate by hurling himself at the stumps in a majestic swallow dive. Inzamam was out by almost six centimetres, and the Pakistan challenge was effectively over.

That dramatic run-out did more than knock the stuffing out of Pakistan: it created the legend of Jonty Rhodes. For the record, South Africa won the match by 20 runs to set up an eventual semi-final against England.

Rhodes took 105 catches in 245 ODIs – an average of just over two per match: an extraordinary performance by an outfielder.

The Golden Eagle

Comparisons were inevitably made between Rhodes and another great South African fielder, Colin Bland, whose exploits in the field earned him the nickname the 'Golden Eagle'.

Like Rhodes 30 years later, Bland was extremely fit, following a Canadian Air Force fitness programme. During South Africa's tour of England in 1964/65, Bland was at his peak, prompting the *Daily Mirror* to describe him as 'superhuman'.

In the first Test at Lord's on 22 July 1965, Bland ran out Ken Barrington and Jim Parks at critical stages of England's first innings to turn the match in South Africa's favour. Barrington was looking comfortable on 91 when he steered the ball wide of mid-on, and cantered off for what he thought was an easy single. Bland swooped from mid-wicket, gathered, turned and hit the stumps from side-on. Parks, on 32, realised he was stranded and tried to get his body in the way of the ball as Bland unleashed a thunderbolt which knocked the middle stump clean out of the ground. The rain-interrupted match ultimately ended in a draw.

During the county match against Kent in Canterbury, Bland gave a fielding demonstration which was captured by the TV cameras. Three stumps were set up in front of a net. Six balls were rolled one by one to Bland. With his first throw, he knocked the stumps sideways; the next two were close misses; the fourth throw knocked two stumps out of the ground, while the fifth knocked the remaining stump down.

Rising to the whisky challenge

Herschelle Gibbs admits he'll try anything, and when the whisky company Johnnie Walker offered a million dollars to a charity if a batsman could hit six sixes in one over in a one-day international, Gibbs was up to the challenge. The extraordinary feat came during South Africa's World Cup match against the Netherlands in Basseterre, St Kitts, on 16 March 2007. South Africa had lost AB de Villiers off the second ball of the match, but then started taking the Dutch bowling apart. Graeme Smith departed for 67 off 59 balls, and Gibbs joined Jacques Kallis at the wicket. Just over three-quarters of an hour later, Gibbs was out for 72, scored off 40 balls, which included four fours and seven sixes.

Six of those sixes came off the hapless Daan van Bunge's fourth over. The word had come out to the middle that Kallis and Gibbs could have a go at the Johnnie Walker challenge, and Gibbs started off with a six over long-on and two over long-off. The fourth ball was a low full toss which went sailing over the mid-wicket boundary. Gibbs then swat-pulled a short-pitched delivery over wide long-off, before bludgeoning the final ball over deep mid-wicket.

Gibbs became the first batsman to score six sixes in one over in ODI cricket.

The previous record for most runs in an over was 30, twice achieved by Sanath Jayasuriya. His seven sixes in the innings was one less than Ricky Ponting's World Cup record of eight.

Mark Boucher was also in fine form, notching up the fastest half-century in World Cups in just 21 balls. He slammed 75 from 31 balls.

South Africa's total of 353 for 3 is their highest World Cup score and the best total in a 40-over match. The 18 sixes hit in the match is also an ODI record.

This was also the first time there were three century stands in a single innings of a one-day international. After AB de Villiers's second-ball dismissal, Graeme Smith and Jacques Kallis added 114 for the second wicket; Kallis and Herschelle Gibbs put together 105 for the third; while Kallis and Boucher added 134 for the fourth.

South Africa won the match by 221 runs. Spare a thought for Van Bunge, who conceded 56 runs from his four overs without taking a wicket.

After the match, Gibbs, then known as a notorious party animal, was asked, 'Herschelle, at what stage did you realise it was a million dollars and not a million bottles of Johnnie Walker that was up for grabs?' This was asked of a man who had once credited a return to form to 'a pizza and a couple of Jack Daniels'.

A double ton and ten sticks at Lord's

No fewer than 22 South Africans are listed on the honours board at Lord's in London, which commemorates a century or five wickets at the home of cricket. South Africa has been particularly dominant in Test matches against England at Lord's in the post-isolation era, with Kepler Wessels and Allan Donald making the honours board in July 1994, and Donald repeating the feat along with Jonty Rhodes in June 1998.

But the most extraordinary feats by South Africans at Lord's were surely Graeme Smith's 257 and the ten-wicket haul by Makhaya Ntini in the second Test in July/August 2003. Ntini was the first to achieve an honours board accolade in the match, when he took 5 for 75 to peg England back to 173 all out in their first innings.

Then Smith took the spotlight. He followed his South African Test record score of 277 and 85 in the first Test at Edgbaston with the highest score for his country at Lord's. His 257, scored in just over nine and a half hours, included 34 fours. He became the second South African to score two double hundreds against England, and equalled the great Don Bradman's record of a double century in consecutive Tests against them. He also joined an illustrious group – Bradman, Wally Hammond and Vinod Kambli – the only players to hit double tons in successive matches. Gary Kirsten also added his name to the honours board with a score of 108, as South Africa declared at 682 for 6. The senior pro shed a tear, knowing this had been his last chance to get on the honours board, as this would be his final tour of England before retiring.

Back came Ntini, and after a tussle with the obstinate Andrew Flintoff (who hit 142 – the highest score by a number seven batsman at Lord's), took 5 for 145. After Andrew Hall had safely pouched the catch to get rid of Steve Harmison, thereby giving Ntini his tenth wicket, the big fast bowler knelt down on the wicket and, in a moment of pure theatre, kissed the ground before raising his arms aloft to acknowledge the appreciative crowd.

He became the first South African to take ten wickets at Lord's and shared the player-of-the-match award with Graeme Smith. South Africa won the match by an innings and 92 runs.

Always one for a quote, Ntini spoke with raw emotion when asked how he felt about his achievement: 'Relief, enjoyment and a lot of pride. All I could think about was the fact that the name "Ntini" would forever sit in the place they call the home of cricket. I thought of my children seeing their name on the wall one day, and then I thought of all the young black boys who would know that anything is possible. But I was just glad to put a South African name up there because I wanted every South African to share my pride.'

An unprecedented four South Africans made the honours

board in July 2008 in the drawn Test at Lord's – Ashwell Prince (101), Graeme Smith (107), Neil McKenzie (138) and Hashim Amla (104).

D'Oliveira leads South Africa against Kenya

In the 1956/57 season, a visit to South Africa by Peter May's England team captured the sports headlines. However, another tour of significance took place in South Africa which received almost no mainstream media attention – by the Kenyan Asians. The tour was organised by the South African Cricket Board of Control. The Kenyan team included six players with first-class experience in India and Pakistan, and included Shakoor Ahmed, who had played for Pakistan in England two years earlier.

The tourists played three 'Tests' against a South African XI captained by a 25-year-old Basil D'Oliveira. The South Africans won the first match on matting at the Hartleyvale Football Ground by six wickets, with D'Oliveira scoring 70 in the first innings to steady the ship after the openers had gone cheaply. He then guided his team to victory, hitting the winning runs in a knock of 36 not out in the second innings. In the second match in Natalspruit, Johannesburg, South Africa won by 39 runs. The third match, played at Kingsmead in Durban, ended in a draw. D'Oliveira headed the averages with an impressive 53.

Two years later, D'Oliveira led a team to tour Kenya in August 1958. The South Africans started slowly owing to a lack of match practice, as the tour came at the end of the off season. But eight weeks later, they had won 13 of their 16 matches, including the two 'Tests' against Kenya. Again, D'Oliveira showed his remarkable talents, scoring 139 in the second innings of the first unofficial Test at the Sikh Union Club Ground in Nairobi, after a first innings duck, to steer his team to a 165-run win. The innings was regarded as one of the finest of D'Oliveira's career. The match also produced a great bowling performance from Eric Petersen, a notorious reveller. He arrived in the morning without having slept, bedraggled and smelling of booze. An enraged D'Oliveira threatened to send him home, but his teammates persuaded him to let Petersen play. The tall fast bowler knew he had to do something special to save his place in the team, and tore into the Kenyan batting to take 6 for 51 in Kenya's first innings.

In a moment of irony during the match, the South African players stood on the field for a minute of silence to mark the death of the South African Prime Minister JG Strijdom, the man whose government had authorised the destruction of District Six, where many of the players lived, and whose racial policies meant they couldn't join their white counterparts in official Test cricket.

In the second unofficial Test at the Mombasa Sports Club Ground in September 1958, a half-century by D'Oliveira helped his side to a 255-run win. Petersen was again unplayable, taking 5 for 14 in the Kenya first innings and 4 for 29 in the second. Between the two unofficial Tests, D'Oliveira's team beat a combined East African team by seven wickets in Nairobi, with the captain scoring 96 in the second innings.

Bringing it up with a six

Paul Winslow was not enjoying the most memorable of Test careers when he played in his fourth Test for South Africa against England in Manchester in July 1955, the third Test of the series. But his knock of 108 in South Africa's first innings of that match gave him a place in the history books. Coming in at number seven, he started slowly, but after lunch he set about the England attack. At one stage of his innings, he scored 42 off 12 balls.

The shot that took him to his maiden first-class century is the one that will always be remembered. Facing England's spin bowler Tony Lock, with 94 to his name and South Africa's score on 399, the bespectacled Winslow brought up his 100 and South Africa's 400 with one of the biggest sixes ever seen at Old Trafford. The straight drive landed on the roof of the stands before bouncing into a neighbouring practice ground, where it was retrieved by a policeman. Winslow was out eight runs later.

South Africa won the match by three wickets with just minutes to spare on the final day. John Waite was batting with a rather dusty Hugh Tayfield, who had fallen over trying to hit Lock out of the park. With four runs needed and five minutes left on the clock, Waite finally drove the ball into an open space and it limped over the boundary as the players turned for the winning run.

Cook carries his bat twice in a game

Jimmy Cook was the stalwart batsman for Transvaal in the 'Mean Machine' era of the 1980s, and carried this form over to England where he played county cricket for Somerset. He made sure he would be remembered by repeating a feat first achieved in 1911, and not achieved subsequently.

Back in 1911, Cecil Wood carried his bat twice in the same match. Playing for Leicestershire against Yorkshire in Bradford in June 1911, Wood made 107 not out and 117 not out. Wood was either a remarkable player or he played in teams with mediocre batting line-ups because he managed this feat 17 times in his career. But after that performance against Yorkshire, no batsman carried his bat twice in an innings in English county cricket – until July 1989, when Jimmy Cook arrived at the wicket for Somerset against Nottingham at Trent Bridge. He scored 120 not out and 131 not out as Somerset were beaten by an innings and 67 runs. The next highest score in each innings was 21 and 50. With all the other batsmen failing (there were five ducks in Somerset's second innings), Cook's contribution amounted to 64.5% of the first-innings tally and 60.1% of the second-innings score. Not since 1956 had a batsman made more than 60% of his side's total in both innings in a first-class match. At a later match, Cook was asked by a spectator to sign a particular page in a book. The only other signature on that page was that of the man whose extraordinary feat he had emulated – Cecil Wood.

The remarkable maiden over

South African bowler Andrew Hall bowled one of the most extraordinary final overs of a one-day international to give his side victory over Sri Lanka in Adelaide on 24 January 2006. Playing in the sixth match of the triangular VB Series, Sri Lanka needed 11 runs off the final over, chasing 264 to win the match. Hall had the task of bowling the over, and he achieved something that no other bowler had done in ODI cricket: he bowled a maiden over. His effort was even more extraordinary in that he bowled three of the balls to the prodigious hitter Tillakaratne Dilshan, who had already scored 82 from 108 balls and had his eye in. Also at the wicket was Muttiah Muralitharan, but all the two Sri Lankans were able to do was scramble a leg bye. South Africa won the match by nine runs.

Hall is surely the only international cricketer who survived being shot at point-blank range in an attempted mugging at an autobank machine. The incident occurred in 1998, a year before he made his ODI debut. A gunman fired six shots at him. One bullet hit him in the left hand, but didn't cause serious damage. Another grazed his cheek and he got a piece of shrapnel in his eye. Hall went on to play 21 Tests and 88 ODIs for South Africa.

A score of 258 for a 12-year-old girl

Scoring 258 in a schools cricket match is considered pretty good, but for one player to score that many runs in a 40-over match defies belief. It happened in a provincial under-13 match between Gauteng North and Gauteng played at the Grayston Primary School in Sandton on 22 November 2002. The batsman, errh ... *batswoman* ... was a 12-year-old schoolgirl, Mignon du Preez. Her knock, according to Mignon's recollection included 28 fours and 16 sixes, though some records say she hit 25 fours. What's not disputed is that Mignon faced 98 balls, which means she had a strike rate of over two and a half runs per ball. Mignon wasn't supposed to play in the game, but got a late call-up when Gauteng North realised they were a player short. She guided her team to a total of 350 and victory by 274 runs. Mignon started playing cricket at the age of four, when her brother's mini-cricket side found themselves a player short during a tournament in Laudium. Despite playing against children four or five years older than herself, Mignon went on to win the award for best batsman of the day, and her cricket career started. At the age of eight, Mignon played junior club cricket for a boy's team, and the following year was picked for the Gauteng North girls under-13 team at the age of nine.

Mignon went on to play for the national under-19 women's cricket team and later for the national squad, making her ODI debut in January 2007 against the Pakistan women's side. She represented South Africa at the ODI World Cup in Australia in 2009 and the Twenty20 World Cup in the West Indies in 2010.

Dolly's big knock

Basil D'Oliveira, playing for Croxley (the stationery company that employed him as a printer) against Mariedahl in Cape Town in 1953/54, scored 225 in 65 minutes, including 28 sixes and ten fours – meaning that he only ran 17 of his runs. He scored his first 100 runs in 25 minutes. The rest of his team scored just 11 runs between them as Croxley scored 236.

In another game, the young D'Oliveira hit 81 for St Augustine against Trafalgar CC, including 46 off one eight-ball over, comprising seven sixes and one four.

Big-hitting Nourse

South African Test cricketer Dudley Nourse, playing for a South African XI against the Military Police in Cairo in 1942, hit nine sixes off consecutive balls, and 11 in 12 balls, an unparalleled feat of fast scoring.

'Guinness' holds the records

Mark Boucher holds practically every South African wicketkeeping record in Tests and one-day internationals.

On the fourth day of the second Test between South Africa

and the West Indies in St Kitts in June 2010, Boucher became the first man to claim 500 Test dismissals, catching an edge from Ravi Rampaul off Morné Morkel. His 500 included 478 catches and 22 stumpings. He is also the only Test wicketkeeper to have scored 5,000 runs and taken 500 dismissals.

It is unlikely that he will be passed for some time, as the closest to him is Adam Gilchrist (416), who has retired from international cricket. Indeed, the next 13 behind him on the list have all retired, so the man with the best chance of overtaking Boucher is Pakistan's Kamran Akmal, with 181 dismissals at the time of writing.

He has been such a prolific record-breaker that he was given the nickname 'Guinness' (as in the *Guinness Book of World Records*).

He started his remarkable run of records as early as his fourth Test match between South Africa and Pakistan in Port Elizabeth in March 1998, equalling his predecessor Dave Richardson's record of nine dismissals in a Test. He took six catches in Pakistan's first innings and a further two plus one stumping in the second innings as South Africa won the match by 269 runs.

Screw turns the screw

After he had ripped through the English batting to almost single-handedly set up South Africa's win in the third Test in Cape Town in January 2005 and level the series at 1-1, Charl Langeveldt was forced out of the team with a broken hand, sustained on the second day.

It did not stop him turning out for his provincial union, the Warriors, in Port Elizabeth in a SuperSport Series match a few days later, and, in what must be a fast bowler's dream, Langeveldt was not allowed to bat lest he damage his broken left hand. He was listed by the scorers as 'absent hurt' for both innings, as the injury had left him incapable of batting. His little finger had been broken.

In what had been Langeveldt's debut Test match, Andrew Flintoff hit him on his left hand in the second last over of the South African innings. On reflection, this was a silly thing for Flintoff to do to a fellow fast bowler – Langeveldt was fired up and tore the English batting apart, taking 5 for 46 in the first innings as England were dismissed for 163. He had Michael Vaughan caught by AB de Villiers for 11, Geraint Jones caught by Graeme Smith for 13, Graham Thorpe caught by Jacques Rudolph for 12, and he bowled Simon Jones and Steve Harmison for ducks.

With Langeveldt having been a former prison guard, there was a suggestion that the headline might have been 'Former screw turns the screw' in some of the English tabloids. Langeveldt admitted to being in 'a lot of pain' and was receiving two anaesthetic injections a day, the first at 3am and the other after the day's play: 'My adrenalin was pumping and I was confident of bowling in the right areas. When the blood's warm, it's warm!'

GREAT MATCHES

Clive Rice's dramatic last ball

One of the most extraordinary conclusions to a Currie Cup cricket match occurred during the New Year's match between Western Province and Transvaal in Cape Town in January 1977. On the final day of a thrilling match, in which Transvaal had declared twice, Western Province were set a target of 252 to get in 80 minutes plus 20 overs. Province's captain Eddie Barlow was never shy of a challenge, and he and André Bruyns set about the Transvaal attack, with Peter Kirsten and Kepler Wessels continuing the onslaught.

As the victory target loomed closer, nervous Province players started losing their wickets. The match came down to the last over, to be bowled by Clive Rice. Province needed eight runs with just two wickets standing. Rice conceded two runs off his first three balls, and then bowled Province paceman Stephen Jones. The tailenders scrambled a leg bye off the fifth ball. Province now needed five runs to win off the final ball of the match, while Transvaal needed one wicket.

Province's wicketkeeper Rob Drummond had to face the last ball. Transvaal captain David Dyer took his time setting the field, creating extra tension for Drummond, who had either to hit a six to secure a win, or not lose his wicket to prevent a defeat. As Rice came charging in, Drummond had made up his mind to block the ball and force the draw. As he stretched forward to Rice's delivery, he thought he had the ball covered, only to hear his stumps clatter behind him. Transvaal had pulled off a remarkable four-run win over their fierce rivals.

In the dressing room after the match, Drummond, a medical

student, went dashing off because he had exams the next day. As he headed out the door, Barlow chirped to him, 'Rob, watch out for the last question.'

Seven runs, one ball – and victory

One of the most extraordinary finishes to a cricket match occurred in a Benson & Hedges semi-final first-leg match between Natal and Transvaal at Kingsmead, Durban, on 13 March 1991. Natal needed seven runs off the last ball for victory and got them. Transvaal set Natal a target of 226 for victory in 45 overs. As Richard Snell prepared to bowl the final over, Natal needed 14 runs to win. Jonty Rhodes and Arthur Wormington managed to get seven runs from the first five balls, leaving Natal with the seemingly impossible tally of seven runs off the last ball. That's when things went horribly wrong. Snell bowled Rhodes a high full toss. Jonty smashed the ball for six and the match was tied. But the square-leg umpire Hennie de Bruyn called a no-ball for height. No extra run was accrued for the no-ball, according to the rules of the day, but an extra ball had to be bowled. Captain Jimmy Cook called the field up to stop the single, but Rhodes hit the ball straight through Steve Smith's hands at short mid-wicket for four to give Natal the unlikely victory.

When the hour comes ...

'When the hour comes, so doth the man' is the quote synonymous with one of the most exciting finishes to a Test match. The match was the first Test between South Africa and England in Durban in December 1948. On the final day, England needed 128 runs in 128 minutes in fading light and with a light drizzle falling. The wet ball was playing havoc with the South Africans in the field and several catches were spilled. The bowlers were also having problems getting a good grip. Nevertheless, wickets tumbled and eventually England needed 12 runs, South Africa needed two wickets and five minutes remained for play. BBC commentator John Arlott summed up the situation: 'Those two wickets can fall as easily as those 12 runs can come.'

England's number ten batsman, Cliff Gladwin, strode to the wicket to join Alec Bedser. He described the events to the *Daily Mail* cricket writer, Alex Bannister:

> As I went to the wicket I passed a grim-faced [South African captain] Dudley Nourse, and as I was grinning, he asked, 'What have you to laugh about?'
>
> I replied, 'When the hour comes, so doth the man.'
>
> I might have been out first ball to McCarthy, but Lindsay Tuckett at mid-on missed a possible chance and, taking a second run, Alec Bedser was nearly run out.
>
> Off the seventh ball we had a misunderstanding. Alec played the ball to Ossie Dawson at short leg, and started to run. I sent him back and Dawson's throw just missed the stumps. Another run from the overthrow.

So to the vital last [eight-ball] over. Eight runs to win and the clock hands pointing to two minutes to six. Lindsay Tuckett to Bedser and as the first ball was a leg bye, I knew, as the striker, it was going to be up to me. I called down the wicket to Alec with false bravery, 'Don't worry, my little champion, we're going to get 'em.'

The next ball I swiped to leg and my heart almost stopped beating as I saw it going straight towards Eric Rowan at deep mid-wicket. Fortunately, however, it sailed over his head for the sweetest boundary of my career.

The third ball went for another leg bye and it was not until the sixth that Alec managed to collect a single, and two balls to go. Alec noticed that Billy Wade, the wicketkeeper, was standing back and called me down the wicket. He said, 'As soon as the ball passes the stumps – run.'

I replied: 'Right.'

But in the excitement I forgot my orders and had to scream to Alec to get back to his crease. Wade was so excited that he could not pick up the ball and had to kick it to a fielder.

The last ball came up and I thought, as Tuckett approached the wicket, 'If only I can get out of this alive!'

I saw the ball distinctly but it was too quick to connect and it hit my thigh. I heard Alec positively screaming, 'Run, run!' I ran all right, as if my shirt was on fire, and after gaining my ground, waved my bat in the air and did a dance of triumph.

Amid all the drama, the umpire forgot to signal a leg bye, and the matter had to be rectified after the game.

It was one of the most dramatic finishes to a Test match in South Africa, but in an era when people followed cricket on the radio, it was also a finish that most South African cricket fans missed. The SABC was so strict about crossing to the news bulletin promptly at 6pm that the commentary was cut as Tuckett was coming in to bowl the final delivery so that the news could start on time. Listeners missed out on the leg bye and England's famous victory.

Don't stand so close to me

Seldom have cricket matches been won and lost because a player was standing in the wrong place, but that's what happened in a dramatic match between Transvaal and Natal at the Wanderers in December 1967. Transvaal needed a gettable 58 runs in just under two and a half hours, but there was urgency to Eddie Barlow and Albie During's batting as large, dark Highveld storm clouds were rapidly approaching the ground. During lost his wicket for ten runs, and then a vanguard rainstorm hit the Wanderers for ten minutes, as if to prepare the ground for the impending deluge.

There was a brief lull in the weather before the inevitable storm, and in the gathering dark, Ali Bacher lost his wicket for six. The rain was holding off, and the next batsman, Ray White, sprinted to the wicket to join Barlow. Barlow knew he only had minutes before the Wanderers would be engulfed in rain, and hit two successive fours to tie the game. Huge, heavy drops of rain started to fall with increasing frequency, accompanied by a cold blast of air across the ground – the precursor to the eventual torrential hailstorm that was now seconds away.

Transvaal needed one run for victory as Mike Procter started his extraordinary long run-up from the golf course end. The Natal captain Berry Versfeld stopped him and moved to a different position behind the batsman at backward short leg to prevent a bye or a quick single from a glancing leg-side shot. The crowd howled in protest, accusing Versfeld of time wasting.

As Procter came steaming in, the rain and hail started pelting down on the old pavilion tin roof, creating such a racket that the players could not hear themselves talk. And, critically, they could not hear Barry Richards, fielding at fine leg, shouting, 'Stop, stop!' Richards had noticed that Barlow, at the non-striker's end, was not backing up as Procter moved in. Richards quickly realised that the wily Barlow had a reason for not wanting to sneak the vital, match-winning run. Barlow knew that a no-ball, and consequently an extra run, was imminent.

Procter unleashed a snorter, at which White could only flay and hope for the best in the dark and amid the noise, and he was bowled. Some Natal players whooped for joy, believing they had held on for the draw, while others stormed off to the safety of the dressing room. White was also heading back, while the incoming batsman, Richard Dumbrill, came sprinting to the wicket.

Barlow, a metre behind the crease at the non-striker's end, stood rooted to the spot, pointing to the square-leg umpire Jack Warner, who was signalling a no-ball. Versfeld had broken the law which allowed just two leg-side fielders behind the wicket when he became the third fielder on White's leg side. The extra run accruing from the no-ball meant Transvaal were the winners by eight wickets – all because Versfeld was standing in the wrong position. Within seconds, the ground at the Bullring was white with hail and there was no chance of any further play that afternoon. Ray White, the vanquished, became the victor.

Glory at the SCG

South Africa's narrowest Test victory to date was against Australia in the second Test at the Sydney Cricket Ground in January 1994. After being outplayed for four days, and having set Australia a meagre target of just 117 to win the match with a day left, South Africa appeared dead and buried. However, a superb spell of bowling in the late afternoon of the fourth day gave the South Africans some hope.

Fanie de Villiers got rid of Michael Slater in the first 15 minutes of the innings, but Mark Taylor and David Boon consolidated and took the Australians to 51 as the close of play drew near. That's when De Villiers struck again to great effect, getting the wickets of Boon, nightwatchman Tim May for a golden duck and then Mark Taylor five runs later. Australia were knocked back to 63 for 4, but with Mark Waugh and Allan Border still at the crease and Damien Martyn, Ian Healy and Shane Warne still to come, they felt quite confident of knocking off the 54 runs for victory on the final day.

In fact, so confident of a quick end were the SCG authorities that they announced the next day's entrance would be free in order to attract something of a crowd. Twelve thousand people pitched up that beautiful summer's morning, expecting to see another Australian victory at the SCG, but instead witnessed a great climax to a Test match and an Aussie defeat.

Hansie Cronje was captaining for the first time in the place of the injured Kepler Wessels, who had broken a finger. But Wessels, a former Australian Test player, still played a critical role in the match, working out a strategy to dismiss the veteran Border. He suggested the critical ball to get rid of the wily Australian captain.

Allan Donald pounded in to deliver the second ball of the morning. Border padded up, expecting the ball to move away from him. But it cut back off the seam, and flicked off Border's off-stump bail. He stood bewildered and disbelieving as the South Africans screamed an appeal, and the wicketkeeper, Dave Richardson, urgently pointed out the fallen bail to the hesitant umpires. Border was out without adding to his score, and the biggest psychological blow had been struck. From then on, the Australian batsmen were nervous as they started a famous choke.

Australia were now rocking at 63 for 5. Waugh had battled for almost an hour, fending off a fired-up Donald, and De Villiers toiling away from the other end. Waugh added just seven more runs before Donald trapped him LBW. Australia were 72 for 6. Healy came and went as De Villiers smashed a ball into his stumps with only one run added to the total. Australia's last recognised batsman, Shane Warne, came to the wicket, with Australia requiring 44 for victory and South Africa needing three wickets.

Cronje has never received the proper credit for his brilliant run-out to get rid of Warne – he chased down a ball heading for the boundary, picked it up and performed a pirouette that Nijinsky would have applauded. He hurled a pinpoint throw on the turn to the wicket, hitting one of the stumps. A scrambling Shane Warne stood no chance, as he was halfway down the wicket. Eight down with 42 still needed and Australia were well and truly into the tail as Craig McDermott joined Martyn at the wicket.

While Martyn had been scratching around for half an hour without getting off the mark, McDermott decided to attack the close-in field. He cracked four fours over the cordon as he and Martyn put on 35 runs – 29 of them by McDermott. The pendulum appeared to be swinging back Australia's way.

Martyn's luck finally ran out when he pulled a snorter from Donald into the safe hands of Andrew Hudson at cover. On 110 for 9, Australia needed seven runs; South Africa needed one wicket. Glenn McGrath, playing in his third Test match, with nine Test runs to his name – all scored in Australia's first innings – walked nervously to the wicket. The clock was slowly approaching 1pm and lunch. The South Africans were desperate to finish the job while they had the momentum.

McGrath had added one more run to the total when Fanie de Villiers started what would be the final over before lunch. McGrath fended off the first two deliveries, but on the third ball of the over, he prodded one straight back to De Villiers, who snatched at the return catch with two eager hands. He threw the ball high into the sky, uttering a bellow that could be heard around the ground. He stood rigid to the spot in his sheer joy, knees bent and tightening his biceps while his teammates engulfed him.

South Africa had won the match by five runs – their narrowest Test victory yet, and achieved at the hallowed Sydney Cricket

Ground against the mighty Australians. De Villiers was awarded man of the match for his figures of 10 for 123. De Villiers reminded Tony Greig in the post-match TV interview that he (Greig) had given South Africa odds of 100-1 to win at the start of the final day. De Villiers also reminded the former South African cricketer: 'You know South Africans; we never give up.'

Two hat-tricks

The matches played during the so-called 'rebel' series between South Africa and Australia of 1985/86 and 1986/87 are recognised as first-class matches, but not officially as Test matches. So many extraordinary events occurred in the third and final match in Johannesburg in January 1986. The South African XI won the match by 188 runs, dismissing the Australian XI for just 61 in their second innings. The fact that two brothers, Ossie and Dudley Schoof, umpired the match was unusual enough, but far bigger things were to happen.

The luckless Kim Hughes joins the list of the great non-performers in cricket history with a king pair (a golden duck in each innings). Then he came out as a runner for the injured Rodney Hogg, who was promptly bowled first ball, to give Hughes an unusual hat-trick of golden ducks. The Australian wicketkeeper Steve Rixon took a remarkable ten catches in the match, which equalled the Test record set by England wicketkeeper Bob Taylor in the first Test against India in Bombay in November 1981.

The Australian opener John Dyson scored 18 not out and carried his bat in Australia's second innings of 61, which would have broken Bernard Tancred's 1889 record of 26 not out for the lowest score by a batsman carrying his bat through a completed Test innings. And there was yet more drama as two South African bowlers took hat-tricks in the match. Garth le Roux bowled Greg Shipperd, had Hughes caught behind by Ray Jennings and then trapped Michael Taylor LBW in three successive balls of one over.

Clive Rice's hat-trick was a bit more spread out. He trapped Carl Rackemann LBW and bowled Rodney Hogg in successive deliveries to wrap up the Australian first innings. When he bowled for the first time in the Australian second innings, Rice clean bowled Graham Yallop – his third wicket in three balls – for the second hat-trick.

The 438 game

There are few sporting events known simply by a number, but the fifth ODI of Australia's tour to South Africa in Johannesburg on Sunday 12 March 2006 will forever be known as the '438 game'.

In Australia, however, they thought it was going to be remembered as the 434 match. Time differences had meant Australian newspapers had been printed claiming a new world-record score of 434 for the Australians, but television reports were full of the wonder of the Wanderers.

Chris Scott, the Wanderers groundsman, had prepared a belter of a wicket – the sort of strip that makes bowlers whimper, and, with the series 2-2 and one game to play, it was to be a battle of the batsmen.

In the end, it became a battle of the two number three batsmen. First, Ricky Ponting – in a repeat of his tremendous innings in the final of the 2003 World Cup – smashed 164 off 105 balls, and then Herschelle Gibbs belted 175 from 111 balls.

Wisden described Ponting's innings as 'cultured slogging', which is just about a perfect way of describing a knock that included 13 fours and nine sixes. He had come in after Adam Gilchrist and Simon Katich had put on a decent platform of 97 from the first 15 overs before Gilchrist was caught by Andrew Hall off Roger Telemachus for 55 (44 balls; nine fours). Fifteen overs later, when Katich departed for a relatively sedate 79 from 90 balls (nine fours; one six), they had scored a further 119 runs and still had 20 overs left. The South Africans in the packed Bullring began contemplating their navels as much as their beers. It was getting ugly out there.

Mike Hussey and Ponting put on 158 for the third wicket, with Hussey having rocketed to 81 from just 51 balls (nine fours; three sixes), and when Andrew Symonds, who was supposed to be Australia's big hitter, finally strode to the middle, the score was 374 for 3 with three overs and five balls remaining.

Ponting departed to hearty applause from the South Africans as well as the Australians in the crowd with the score on 407, leaving Symonds and Brett Lee to take the total past 400 for the first time in one-day cricket. It seemed unbelievable: 434 for 4.

With his bowlers taking a hammering, Graeme Smith used

seven bowlers as he sought to slow the onslaught down. He even bowled himself for four overs and was the most economical South African, going for just 29 (7.25 runs per over).

Jacques Kallis was punished the worst with 70 from his six overs. There was just one maiden bowled all day – by Roger Telemachus, who was having a good day ... until his last two overs. He had figures of 1 for 47, but brought on at the death, he either got a case of the yips or strived for a little extra pace, and bowled four no-balls in a row in an over that cost 28 runs. His final figures were 10-1-87-2, although he did have the satisfaction of taking Ponting's wicket.

In the dressing room at the break there was some gallows humour from Kallis: 'I reckon this is a 450 pitch, they've fallen 15 runs short.' It brought a laugh from the South Africans and, said Smith, gave them a sense of freedom. The task was massive, but they would perish trying or not try at all; they had all but been written off by the crowd, the commentators and the rest of the cricketing world.

Time, then, for Smith, the captain who prided himself on leading from the front, to show the way. Boeta Dippenaar was bowled by Nathan Bracken for 1 with the second ball of the second over, which was not the worst thing to happen to South Africa on a day they needed to slog instead of accumulate.

Smith and Gibbs then put on a stand – although the phrase 'stand and deliver' may be more appropriate – of 187 from 121 balls. In the stands, South Africans began to believe and suddenly there was a flicker of doubt amongst the Australians.

Mickey Arthur had set the South Africans a target of 185 from

25 overs to give his side a chance, but South Africa surpassed this and were 229 for 2 halfway through the game.

Smith scored 90 from just 55 balls (13 fours; two sixes), and, when another ODI century seemed all but assured, was caught by Hussey on the mid-wicket boundary off Michael Clarke. South Africa were well in the game at this stage, reported *Wisden*:

> Hussey's celebrations were manic and betrayed the creeping sense of foreboding that had taken hold of Australia's players. Just as South Africa had suffered for the absence of Shaun Pollock, so too was Glenn McGrath's constricting influence being missed. His understudies were simply not up to the task, with Mick Lewis earning an unwanted place in history as his ten overs were spanked for 113 runs – the most expensive analysis in any form of one-day international cricket.

Poor Mick Lewis. In Durban, in the fourth ODI just two days before, he had scored the winning runs as Australia evened the series with one to play. He was the first person to concede 100 runs in a 50-over one-day international. This was no place for a bowler at the death and when he returned home shortly after the Wanderers, he was mobbed by the media at the airport, wanting to share his pain.

But Lewis's failure was overshadowed by the success of Gibbs. As *Wisden* put it:

> Now it was Gibbs who took centre stage. The man who, memorably, dropped the World Cup at Headingley in that 1999 campaign has redeemed himself a hundred times over in the intervening years.

But this was to be his crowning glory. With AB de Villiers providing a sparky sidekick, Gibbs carved great chunks out of the asking-rate, bringing up his century from 79 balls and rattling along so briskly that, by the 25-over mark, South Africa had 229 for 2 on the board, and needed a mere 206 to win.

Perhaps the decisive moment of the match was when Bracken dropped a dolly of a catch off Gibbs at mid-off as the South African mistimed a full toss off the unfortunate Lewis. Bracken was the best bowler of the match with his five wickets for 67 runs from his ten overs, but putting down a rampant Gibbs seemed to suck the life out of the Australians.

Gibbs was finally caught by Lee at long off from a Symonds delivery, having hit 21 fours and seven sixes in his two hours and 22 minutes at the crease.

Kallis and Mark Boucher put on 28 in six overs, but when Kallis was caught and bowled by Symonds for 20 and Justin Kemp toe-ended a wide delivery to Damien at backward point, South Africa looked to have stumbled.

Johan van der Wath, the Free State all-rounder, scored a quick-fire 35 from 18 balls and when he was done, South Africa needed 36 from 22. Telemachus, never afraid to swing a bat, hit two boundaries in his innings of 12, taking just six balls.

And so (reported *Wisden*), it all came down to the final over, just as it had done at Edgbaston all those years ago. Brett Lee had seven runs to defend, and South Africa had two wickets in hand. A blazed four from Andrew Hall seemed to have settled the issue, but in a moment reminiscent of Lance Klusener's famous aberration, he smeared the very next delivery into the hands of Clarke at mid-on. Two runs needed then, and the number 11, Makhaya Ntini, on strike. Lee's best effort was deflected to third man to tie the scores, and it was left to Boucher – with visions of Edgbaston swirling through his head – to seal the deal with a lofted four over mid-on. The most breathtaking game in one-day history had come to a grandstand finish, and all that remained was for the participants to pinch themselves.

The records tumbled on that sunny Sunday in Jo'burg:

- The 438 for 9 was the highest total in an ODI; it needed to be, as the previous record had been set some four hours before.
- It was the most successful chase in ODI history and was the second time Australia had lost an ODI to a record chase, having conceded 332 to New Zealand in Christchurch in December 2005.
- The total of 872 runs was the highest match aggregate of any ODI, beating the 693 totalled by India and Pakistan in Karachi, 2004.
- Poor Mick Lewis's figures of 113 for none from his ten overs were the most expensive in an ODI and the first time someone had gone for more than 100 in a 50-over match. Previously, Muttiah Muralitharan had conceded 99 against Australia in a VB Series final in Australia.
- It was the first two-team ODI series Australia had lost since 2002.
- The 87 fours and 26 sixes in the game was a world record.

Run, Allan, run

When Shaun Pollock returned home after the 1999 Cricket World Cup in England, the memory of Allan Donald's infamous run-out in the semi-final still fresh in his memory and the psyche of all South Africans, he attended the Durban July.

'At the race, someone came up and asked me which horse I was going to bet on. I am not a betting man, but this is one of the country's more traditional events, and I usually have a small wager,' said Pollock. 'I really wasn't sure which horse I was going to put my money on, so I told the man that I didn't know yet. He offered me some advice: "Whatever you do, don't bet on number ten. He doesn't run." I knew that was a reference to Allan Donald not running in the semi-final against Australia. I knew we wouldn't be able to escape the jokes about our semi-final mishap for a while.

'I don't remember which horse I bet on, but what I do know is that number ten, El Picha, won the race, and I hadn't bet on it.'

South Africa and Australia have played in some of the most exciting ODI matches in the history of the shorter form of the game, and, as gripping as the '438 game' may have been, none has yet touched the drama of the 1999 World Cup semi-final at Edgbaston on June 17. No game has had more twists or turns, more genius, more tension and such a bizarre ending. It was, is, will be the greatest ODI match.

The usually staid *Wisden*, in its write-up of the match, said as much: 'This was not merely the match of the tournament: it must have been the best one-day international of the 1,483 so far played. The essence of the one-day game is a close finish, and this was by far the most significant to finish in the closest way of all – with both teams all out for the same score. But it was a compressed epic all the way through, and it ended in a savage twist.'

But there was a long and convoluted tale before that last act – the final twist – was to be played out. The end result of the match was that South Africa were knocked out of the semi-finals of the World Cup for a second time (there was a third occasion in 2007), losing out to Australia, who had finished higher in the Super Six table than they had. South Africa had a better run rate than Australia, but the rules had been set and the men in green and gold had to leave.

Hansie Cronje won the toss and decided to field under heavy skies in Birmingham, on a ground where both Pollock and Donald had played county cricket for Warwickshire.

It proved an inspired move, as Pollock got Mark Waugh to edge the fifth ball of the innings behind to Mark Boucher. From that wicket on, the match was an arm wrestle as the momentum changed hands some six times. Ricky Ponting helped Australia recover with 37 off 48 balls, but then he fell, followed by Darren Lehmann (1) and Adam Gilchrist (20), and South Africa were back on top at 68 for 4. Steve Waugh (56) and Michael Bevan (65) put on a partnership of 90, and at 158 for 6 in the 40th over, Australia were on top again. They scored just 55 for the final 120 overs and were all out for 213 with four balls remaining.

Donald (10-1-32-4) and Pollock (9.2-1-36-5) bowled superbly with economical back-up from Jacques Kallis (10-2-27-1), who was quick and accurate despite struggling with a stomach injury.

South Africa's reply started off brightly enough, but then Shane

Warne produced another miracle ball – a replica of the one he had bowled to Mike Gatting in the Ashes some years before – to dismiss Herschelle Gibbs for 18. Gary Kirsten was bowled two overs later by Warne for 30 and when Cronje was caught by Mark Waugh off Warne for a duck and Daryll Cullinan was run out by Bevan for 6, South Africa were in trouble at 61 for 4. Warne's first eight overs went for 12 runs, but he found sterner competition in Jacques Kallis, whose solid 53 from 92 balls gave South Africa hope.

Jonty Rhodes swung the game back South Africa's way with a scampered 43 from 55 balls, but when Pollock (20), Boucher (5) and Steve Elworthy (5) fell, it was left to Lance Klusener and Donald. They needed 16 to win and had eight balls to do it in.

Klusener cracked a six in the second last over, which was parried over the boundary by Paul Reiffel, and South Africa needed nine from the last six balls.

Damien Fleming was to bowl it, an experienced death bowler who had shown courage in taking the final over in the 1996 World Cup semi-final against the West Indies.

Steve Waugh wanted Fleming to bowl Klusener yorkers a foot just outside the off stump, hoping to cramp his free-swinging arms hitting to his favoured leg side. The first two balls went for four and the scores were tied at 213. Klusener hit the next one to Lehmann and Donald set off for the run, but was sent back. Lehmann missed the run-out chance. South Africa needed one run from three balls, one wicket remaining. Fleming recalled what happened next: 'After Lehmann's miss the batsmen didn't chat and a few guys said Klusener was asking the umpire what the score was. The scores were tied and the pressure seemed to be back on the batsmen. The final ball was the perfect yorker, Klusener mis-hit it and I sensed he was running, but Donald stayed. Fortunately, the ball went to Mark Waugh, who was running in from mid-off, and he flicked it back to me. I did a slow underarm down the pitch and Adam Gilchrist waited and waited.'

Klusener ran, Donald started, stopped, dropped his bat and then started again, but stopped in despair as Gilchrist knocked off the bails. It was the worst of games for South Africa, but the best of games for cricket.

BIZARRE TALES

The splinter that caused all the trouble

A remarkable incident of a batsman being given out 'hit wicket' occurred in the second Test between South Africa and Australia in Johannesburg in November 1921. When Billy Zulch came out to open the South African first innings, the Australian fielders pointed out to Zulch that the shoulder of his bat was cracked. Instead of getting a new bat, Zulch decided to carry on with the damaged bat.

With his score on 4, Zulch fended off a sharply rising ball from the Australian paceman Ted McDonald. The ball hit the cracked shoulder of the bat, dislodging a large splinter of wood which knocked off one of the bails. Law 35 read with Law 28 states that a batsman is out hit wicket if a bail is knocked off the stumps by 'any part of his equipment becoming detached from his person'. The drafters of the laws probably hadn't considered a part of the equipment becoming detached from the equipment itself, but the umpires decided that it was a strong enough case, and Zulch was given out. As he left the field, he suddenly turned back to the wicket to the cheers of the crowd, who thought he had been recalled. But Zulch realised he had made a mark in cricket trivia history, and was merely returning to retrieve a souvenir for himself – the splinter that had caused all the trouble.

Dangerous cracks end play

It's common for cricket matches to be called off because of rain or bad light, but in December 1994 a match between Boland and New Zealand at the newly opened Boland Park was called off 'in the interest of safety'. The decision came on the second day of the match. Large cracks had appeared in the pitch on the first day, resulting in the ball moving around sharply and bouncing alarmingly. Boland batted first and scored just 83; New Zealand replied with 86. Boland returned for their second innings, reaching 31 for 2 at the close. Only five batsmen reached double figures.

When the players returned for the second day, umpires Cyril Mitchley and Brian Jerling decided that the cracks were making the playing conditions so unpredictable and dangerous that the match should be called off for the safety of the batsmen.

Everyone gets to bowl

The scorecard of the fourth Test between the West Indies and South Africa at St John's, Antigua, in April/May 2005 has the extraordinary entry of all 11 South African players bowling in the West Indies first innings. After South Africa had declared on 588 for 6, the West Indians batted for just over 15 and a half hours to score 747 all out – their highest tally against South Africa and third highest in their Test history, with Chris Gayle scoring 317. Three other players scored centuries, although the West Indies' most prolific batsman, Brian Lara, could only manage a surprising four runs.

In a bid to break resilient partnerships, or, as Cricinfo preferred to put it, 'in an effort to stop someone wandering off to the local rum shop in search of a more interesting way of spending the final afternoon of the series', captain Graeme Smith gave all his players a bowl, including wicketkeeper Mark Boucher, who was brought on to try and get the final wicket while AB de Villiers took the gloves. Boucher conceded six runs with his first seven deliveries, and then took his maiden Test wicket when Dwayne Bravo was caught by Ashwell Prince for 107 to end the innings. De Villiers had taken the two previous wickets to fall, those of Daren Powell and Tino Best, for figures of 2 for 49 off 21 overs before taking the gloves. It is surely the only Test match in which two players from the same side played wicketkeeper and bowled, each taking a wicket. The match ended in a predictable draw, though it also set a record for the most centuries in a Test match – eight (De Villiers 114, Smith 126, Kallis 147, Prince 131, Gayle 317, Sarwan 127, Chanderpaul 127 and Bravo 107).

Twenty bowlers – but not twenty wickets

In the third Test between South Africa and England in Cape Town in January 1965, 20 bowlers were used for the first time in a Test match. In England's first innings, South Africa's captain

Trevor Goddard used six bowlers. South Africa piled on the runs in the second innings, but the match was petering out into a draw. England's captain Mike Smith used ten bowlers as the final sessions became more and more meaningless. The only person who didn't get a bowl was wicketkeeper Jim Parks, while part-time bowlers like Geoff Boycott and Ken Barrington leapt at the chance to show off other skills and both returned their best Test match bowling figures – Boycott 3 for 47, Barrington 3 for 4.

With England requiring an impossible 406 for victory, Goddard decided to use the four players who had not bowled in the first innings, with the exception of wicketkeeper Denis Lindsay. Colin Bland, Graeme Pollock, Tony Pithey and Derek Varnals each had two overs, with Barrington impersonating a batsman of times gone by as the match ended on a humorous though ultimately farcical note, with only the wicketkeepers not getting a chance to bowl.

The ball that passed through the stumps

An extraordinary incident occurred during the third Test between Pakistan and South Africa at Faisalabad in October 1998, when a ball bowled by Mushtaq Ahmed to Pat Symcox passed between the off and middle stumps without dislodging the bails. South Africa were struggling at 98 for 7 when Symcox joined Gary Kirsten at the wicket. The googly from Mushtaq shot under Symcox's bat and between the stumps. Some accounts of this remarkable event suggest that the bails had fused to the stumps in the searing heat, but the more likely explanation is that the stumps were planted too loosely in the ground and had tilted over, leaving enough space for the ball to pass through.

The amazing incident was significant in the outcome of the match, as Kirsten and Symcox went on to score 124 for the eighth wicket, with Symcox scoring 81. Kirsten finished on 100 not out, to become the first South African Test batsman since Jackie McGlew in 1953 in Wellington, New Zealand, to carry his bat. South Africa won the Test by 53 runs, and Symcox was named man of the match – if not for his incredible good fortune, then for his 3 for 8 in the second innings and knocks of 81 and 55.

Sibling rivalry

There are many occasions when brothers have been on the same side in an international cricket match. For South Africa, the most famous are Peter and Gary Kirsten (admittedly, they are half-brothers), Peter and Graeme Pollock, Albie and Morné Morkel, David and Tony Pithey, Eric and Athol Rowan and Philip and Reginald Hands. More extraordinary, however, is an instance of brothers being on opposing sides in a Test match. This occurred in a Test between South Africa and England in Cape Town in March 1892, when Frank Hearne made his debut for South Africa against his brothers, Alec and George, who were making their debuts for England. Frank had made his debut for England against South

Africa in Port Elizabeth in March 1889 – South Africa's first ever Test match – and decided to settle in Cape Town after the tour. He started playing for Western Province, and three years later, with very relaxed qualification requirements for a new country, made his debut for South Africa against England, playing against his two brothers and his cousin Jack. Thirty years later, Frank's son George played the first of his three Test matches for South Africa against England in Johannesburg in December 1922.

Going for broke

Two South African Test captains have provided the defining image of a Test match by insisting on playing with a broken hand. Graeme Smith endeared himself to cricket fans around the world – and made his critics choke on humble pie – by coming out to bat in South Africa's second innings in the fourth Test against Australia in Sydney on 7 January 2009. He had suffered a cracked knuckle on his left hand after being struck by a sharply rising ball from Mitchell Johnson, which forced him to retire hurt in South Africa's first innings. Unable to dress himself or pad up, he was called on to bat out eight overs and two balls in South Africa's second innings to force a draw. Smith wasn't expecting to bat, and arrived in the dressing room having to borrow a shirt from Jacques Kallis and a hamburger-stained jersey from Paul Harris. He exchanged his plaster cast for a glove, and joined Makhaya Ntini at the wicket to tumultuous cheers from the appreciative Sydney Cricket Ground crowd. For 26 minutes, Smith held firm against the onslaught from Johnson and Peter Siddle, wincing in pain and sharply pulling his injured hand off the bat after each shot. Finally, Johnson produced a ball that jagged back into Smith's stumps to give Australia a dramatic victory – a ball, Smith said later, which 'probably would have got me out, if I had both arms available'.

Smith was the second South African Test batsman to bat at number one and 11 in the same match. The previous South African who had batted at the extreme ends of the batting order in a Test match was 'Ormy' Pearse at the SCG against Australia in the 1910/11 series.

Smith's heroic stand is the second example of a South African captain ignoring the pain and opting to play. During South Africa's tour of England in 1951, captain Dudley Nourse broke his thumb while fielding a cover drive from Tom Graveney in a county match against Gloucestershire at the Ashley Down Ground in Bristol. Three weeks later, with the thumb not yet healed, and pinned in a pliant splint, Nourse won the toss and chose to bat in the first Test against England at Trent Bridge, Nottingham, on 7 June 1951. When the third wicket fell at 189, Nourse, refusing a pain-killing injection in the throbbing thumb for fear it would numb the joint and affect his grip, joined Jack Cheetham at the wicket. He was unable to hold the bat properly, and the thumb was starting to swell with each jarring thud of bat on ball, causing untold agony. But Nourse refused to show any reaction to the pain.

The great sportswriter Sam Merwis wrote about this dramatic innings:

During the lunch interval [Nourse] sat quietly and alone in the deserted dressing room and I slipped down from the press box to see him. I asked him how he felt, and he pointed to his thumb. 'Take a look,' he said. And I shuddered. The thumb was grotesquely misshapen, and the pin had been knocked out. He had already completed his first 100.

'It hurts like hell when the ball merely hits the bat, never mind my playing a stroke,' he said wanly. He was as pale as a sheet.

Then he said, 'I don't want to give the bowlers any encouragement by showing them I'm in pain, otherwise they'll go for the thumb. Cricket can be rather like boxing in some ways,' he went on, 'especially in a Test. When a boxer receives a cut on the eye, his opponent then makes it his target, and this happens in cricket – in a Test anyway – when a batsman is injured and continues to bat. That's why I don't let on in any way that I'm in pain.'

The attendant told me that the pain was so great that Dudley had fainted when he came into the dressing room. 'I revived him and Mr Nourse asked me not to tell anyone that he had fainted, but I think you should ask him as well.'

I asked Dudley, and he smiled tiredly. 'Yes, I passed out,' he admitted, 'but please don't write it. People will think I'm trying to make out that I'm a hero or something.'

Nourse batted through the pain, through the rest of the day, and through most of the following day to score 208 in nine and a quarter hours, including 25 fours. When he was eventually run out shortly before the close on day two, he declared South Africa's first innings on 483 for 9. But the damage had been severe on the thumb, and he heeded the doctor's advice and played no further part in the match. However, his first-innings heroics were enough and South Africa won the match by 71 runs to record their first Test victory in 16 years and only their second in England.

Wisden wrote: 'Undoubtedly the hero was Nourse ... Mere figurescannotconveythemagnitudeof [his]performance ... The whole of that time he batted under a great handicap. The left thumb, which he had broken at Bristol ... gave him severe pain, particularly when he tried to impart any power into his strokes, and the longer he stayed, the more it swelled.'

Nourse's 208 set a new record for the highest Test score by a South African. However, less than two months later, teammate Eric Rowan broke the record with a knock of 236 in the fourth Test at Headingley in Leeds.

Sam Merwis, writing in the *Sunday Times* in 1983, recalled the story of Eric Rowan signing autographs the day after he hit his record 236 against England:

> Hundreds of excited schoolboys and girls had waited patiently for Rowan outside Headingley, and when he arrived in the team bus, they descended on him like a wave of locusts, clamouring for his autograph. He almost disappeared beneath the crush of their bodies. Some officials then tried to chase away the kids, but Rowan stopped them.
>
> 'No,' he told them, 'they've come a long way to get my autograph, and they've been waiting for a long time. The least I can do is to sign my name, even if I get writer's cramp.'
>
> Rowan told the youngsters to form a line, which almost encircled the ground. Rowan began scribbling his name on the books, bats, pieces of paper and anything else thrust at him.
>
> He started with his usual EAB Rowan. Then, as he fought for time, the signature became EA Rowan and later E Rowan. But he

signed for every youngster.

I was an interested witness to this event – the press in those days travelled with the team in one bus – and I asked Rowan why he had gone to so much trouble to sign the autographs.

'It's simple,' he said, 'when you're a supposedly famous sportsman and the kids *don't* ask you for your autograph, that's the time to start worrying about your career. It's definitely on the slide.'

Rowan said in 1951 he signed his autograph for a small Irish boy in Dublin when the Boks were playing Ireland. About 15 years later, Rowan received a phone call from a man in South Africa, who said, 'You probably don't remember me, Mr Rowan, but I was a very small and scared boy who asked you for your autograph when the Springboks were playing at Dublin University. You very kindly signed it and also patted me encouragingly on the shoulder. Well, I never forgot that. I happen to be the head of a big cosmetics company today, and I would like to do business with you . . .'

Said Rowan: 'It doesn't cost anything to sign – and sometimes it even pays.'

Unusual dismissals

There are ten ways of being dismissed in cricket, six of which are the most common – bowled, caught, LBW, run out, stumped and hit wicket. Unusually, two South African cricketers were dismissed in five different ways in their first five Test innings. Pieter van der Bijl began his Test career against England at the Old Wanderers in December 1938, where he was out LBW. In the second Test in

Cape Town in December 1938/January 1939, he was caught in the first innings and he hit his wicket in the second. He was run out in the first innings of the third Test in Durban and then bowled in the second innings.

Hugh Tayfield also managed the unusual achievement of five different dismissals in his first five innings. Playing against Australia in the 1949/50 series, he was LBW and caught in the first Test at Ellis Park in December 1949, stumped and bowled in the New Year's Test at Newlands, Cape Town, and run out in the first innings of the third Test at Kingsmead, Durban.

For the record, the other ways of being dismissed in cricket are: handled the ball, timed out, double hit and obstructing the field. South African wicketkeeper Russell Endean was involved in two of these more unusual dismissals. In the fifth Test between England and South Africa at the Oval in August 1951, England's opener Len Hutton was given out obstructing the field in the second innings after he had prevented Endean from making a catch. A ball from Athol Rowan hit Hutton on the glove and rolled up his arm. Believing that it would fall on his stumps, Hutton tried to swat at the ball, but missed. Endean moved in to take the catch, but had to duck low to avoid Hutton's flailing bat. The swipe prevented Endean from catching the ball. The South Africans appealed and Hutton was given out.

In South Africa's second innings against England in the second Test in Cape Town in January 1957, Endean became the first batsman in Test cricket to be given out 'handled the ball'. Batting in South Africa's second innings, Endean padded away a delivery from Jim Laker. As the ball spun up towards his stumps, Endean palmed the ball away with his right hand. It was an illegal move, and Endean entered the record books as the first Test batsman to be given out this way. Charles Fortune, in his book *The MCC Tour of South Africa 1956–1957*, wrote: 'Endean, the ball gone, did not immediately drop his right arm. He stood half bemused, as though aware that something had gone amiss, if not entirely sure what it was. Laker, equally, was momentarily at a loss. Then slowly, and, I am quite sure, somewhat unhappily, he turned to umpire Costello and very quietly asked his question.' Endean later said: 'I thought of heading it away, but that seemed too theatrical.'

False starts to a Test career

Jacques Rudolph had to endure three false starts before finally making his Test debut. Rudolph was originally scheduled to play in his first Test match when South Africa met India at SuperSport Park on 23 November 2001 in the third Test. But a row erupted after match referee Mike Denness found six Indian players guilty of various offences during the drawn second Test in Port Elizabeth. The Board of Control for Cricket in India demanded that Denness be replaced as referee for the third Test, and threatened to cancel the tour if this didn't happen. The BCCI found an ally in the United Cricket Board of South Africa, but the International Cricket Council opposed them and declared the match unofficial. Rudolph played in the match, but it now had the status of a five-day friendly.

Two months later, Rudolph was once again due to make his Test debut against Australia in Sydney. However, the UCB President, Percy Sonn, objected to the team being 'too white' and replaced Rudolph with Justin Ontong. Rudolph had to wait yet again for his big moment, but there was a further delay when Graeme Smith was considered over him to make his Test debut in the second Test against Australia at Newlands in March 2002.

Rudolph finally played Test cricket, making his debut against Bangladesh in Chittagong in April 2003, 17 months after he had first been selected for his country. He became only the fifth player in history to score a double century on his Test debut, hitting 222 not out.

Don't tempt fate

Superstitious South African players have gone to slightly strange lengths to ward off bad luck. Athol Rowan would always go off to wash his hands while his captain went out for the coin toss. He would also refuse to change a pair of cricket longs if he believed they had brought him a good knock. Even in a Test match, he would wear the same pair, regardless of how muddy the conditions were.

Hugh Tayfield's superstition of removing his cap and kissing the badge before each over began in the second Test in Melbourne in December 1952 when, with the Australian openers Colin McDonald and Arthur Morris grinding out a solid opening partnership, a teammate suggested to him: 'Try something different. Anything. Kiss your cap. Just try something.' Almost immediately, Tayfield had Morris caught and bowled to break the partnership. He went on to take 13 for 165 to set up an 82-run win which helped the South Africans to share their first series in Australia. From then on, Tayfield would fold his cap and kiss the Springbok badge on the front before handing it to the umpire. His ritual also included tapping the toe of his boot on the ground before moving in to bowl – giving him the nickname 'Toey'.

South African leg-spinner Xenophon Balaskas was a key player in South Africa's first Test win in England at Lord's in June/July 1935, helped by a pregnant woman (or so he believed). The night before the start of the match, Balaskas was walking with sportswriter Louis Duffus when they came across Greek Street in Soho. Being the son of Greek migrants, who had opened the first restaurant in Kimberley, Balaskas saw the street as something of an omen. He and Duffus made a detour down the road where they spotted a pregnant woman. 'Now there's luck,' Balaskas exclaimed. 'If I pat her I can't go wrong.' He duly patted the puzzled woman and within the next few days his strange superstition brought him the best performance of his career – 9 for 103, and South Africa won the match by 157 runs. His first wicket was that of Maurice Leyland, who had taunted him after he had bowled a huge leg break: 'Why don't you turn the effing ball, Bally?' So Balaskas bowled him a straight one, which hit Leyland's stumps.

Neil McKenzie used to tape his bat to the ceiling before an innings and always made sure that all the toilet seats in the changing room were down. And when he went out to bat he wasn't overly keen on stepping on the crease lines.

Mark Boucher tells the story of him and McKenzie in their

under-19 days. McKenzie had lugged his coffin off the team bus and up 200 steps to the dressing room. Boucher then opened McKenzie's bag and took out one of his three bats. 'You can't do that; I've got to be the first to touch my bats,' McKenzie exploded. He then packed up the bag, took it down the steps all the way to the coach and carried it back to the dressing room.

The confusing run that never was

Extraordinary confusion occurred in a club match between Balfour Park and Old Johannians in Linksfield. The incident is recounted in umpire Hayward Kidson's autobiography, *Over And Time*. He doesn't give an exact date to the match, though it was probably in 1962/63.

Balfour Park were batting, with Archer Wilson and Ali Bacher at the wicket. Wilson played a ball from Gerald Innes into the covers and he and Bacher went for a quick single. Halfway down the track, Wilson changed his mind and started back to his crease. Bacher was having none of it, and both batsmen arrived at the striker's crease at the same time as the ball. The wicketkeeper put the wicket down and appealed for a run-out, which wasn't given. The wicketkeeper threw the ball down in disgust as both batsmen realised one of them had to get to the other end. The problem was that they both set off, with the slip fielder gathering the ball and throwing it to the bowler, Innes. He dropped the ball and broke the wicket illegally with his hands. Bizarrely, both batsmen then charged back to the striker's end, while Innes frantically tried to re-gather the ball and break the stumps again. He pushed one of them at an angle, holding the ball aloft and appealed. But the bails had already been dislodged and the umpire shook his head. So Innes threw the ball to the wicketkeeper, but Wilson had made his ground, so he was not out. The ball was then thrown back to Innes, who, in his eagerness to catch it, knocked all three stumps out of the ground. He had also fallen over. He quickly got to his feet, planted a stump into the ground and then, with the ball in one hand, pulled the stump out with his other hand and appealed. Bacher had persuaded Wilson to stop running, and he had now made good his ground. No runs had been scored because the batsmen had never crossed, and no one was out, even though all the bails and most of the stumps were on the ground.

Low-flying plane stops play

If the subject of South African sport is discussed along with low-flying aircraft, the topic of conversation would surely be the notorious third rugby Test between the Springboks and the All Blacks in Auckland in 1981, during which an anti-apartheid protester lobbed flour bombs at the players, hitting All Black prop Gary Knight on the head.

However, there's an earlier incident of a low-flying aircraft disrupting South African sportsmen in an international match. This time the sport was cricket. During the first Test between

South Africa and England at the Old Wanderers, on 24 December 1927, two Tiger Moths started buzzing over the ground. One of them dived towards the players, pitching up just metres above the ground. The South African batsmen, Jock Cameron and Bob Catterall, along with the England team suspended play and watched aghast as the plane carried out two more dives before flying off.

The Star newspaper admitted that it may have been at fault, having hired a plane to fly its photographer over the ground for some aerial shots. However, *The Star* was adamant that the pilot didn't fly over the ground. It also pointed out that it had carried an advertisement for a 'Bird's-Eye View of Johannesburg' by the Johannesburg Light Plane Club, which included a flip over the Test match. This was the plane that caused the trouble because, although the authorities had given the flight the all-clear, no one had told the players and no one had told the pilot to behave properly.

Jackers runs a six

Here's a story that may not be about South African cricket exactly, but it is about one of our favourite commentators, Robin Jackman, who played cricket for many years in South Africa in the Currie Cup. Although an all-run four is quite common in cricket, an all-run six is surely unique. 'Jackers' was involved in such an incident in Surrey's Sunday League (40 overs) game against Yorkshire at the Oval on 9 June 1974. *Wisden* just reports that Intikhab Alam and Robin Jackman 'both hit boldly and even ran a six' as they rescued Surrey from 43 for 6 with a stand of 74.

A contributor to Cricinfo.com was at the Oval and gave this fabulous eyewitness account of what happened:

> The wicket was placed ... giving one very long boundary and one quite short one. Jackman was batting at the pavilion end and cut Mike Bore (I think) to third man. He set off at a gallop, as did the fielder when he realised that the ball was not going to cross the boundary. An early example of relay throwing followed, and the relay fielder hurled the ball at the wicketkeeper's end, trying to run out Intikhab Alam, who was going for the third run. Unfortunately the throw was well wide of the mark, defeating David Bairstow and the backing-up fielders. The ball whistled through wide mid-on, and Jackman called for two runs on the overthrow. The fielder at wide mid-on, seeing Intikhab struggling to complete the fifth run, had another go at the wicketkeeper's end, trying to run him out. Another wayward throw went past Bairstow, allowing Jackman to call Intikhab for the sixth run (in spite of the fact that Intikhab had gone well past the stumps) and the second wayward throw was fielded by the fielder who had originally fielded the ball on the third-man boundary, on his way back to his fielding position. This fielder finally managed to return the ball safely to Bairstow. Jackman was out soon after, and actually fell to his knees just in front of the pavilion on his way back to the dressing room, reducing most of the crowd to tears of laughter!

Changing the tide
of Australian politics

Jack Cheetham's Springbok side was vastly underrated when it embarked on the three-month tour of Australia in December 1952. Against all odds, the team drew the series 2-all. One of the youngsters in the side was Roy McLean. During a rigorous fielding practice session before the start of their second tour match against Western Australia at the WACA, McLean saw a man lying on the side of the field. He was a student making extra money as a gardener, and had been spreading compost on a bed of roses at the side of the ground.

He had managed to injure himself severely, having trapped his leg between a fence post and the wheel of a wagon. He had suffered a cut to his leg which was so deep that an artery had been severed and blood was gushing from the wound.

McLean and the team manager, Ken Viljoen, rushed over to help. McLean removed his shirt and he and Viljoen made a makeshift tourniquet with which they were able to staunch the bleeding. The gardener was rushed to hospital where he made a full recovery. The young man was 26-year-old Bob Hawke, who became the 23rd Prime Minister of Australia 31 years later, holding office for eight years. He thanked McLean by hosting him to a dinner.

Frogs stop play

Frogs stopped play in January 1923 at the start of the third Test between South Africa and England in Durban. It had rained overnight and the pitch had been covered. England opener Andy Sandham faced the first ball of the match from Tip Snooke. Surprisingly, the ball slowed remarkably after it had pitched. The same thing happened to the second ball.

A bewildered Sandham went to investigate what was slowing the ball down at the point where Snooke was pitching it. To his amazement, he found a small mound of tiny green frogs. Play was held up while the groundsmen scooped the frogs into a bucket. The incident might have preyed on Sandham's mind, and he was out for a duck shortly afterwards. The rain-interrupted match ended in a draw.

It's worth pointing out that Sandham might have been undone by a pile of frogs, but in his final Test match against the West Indies in Kingston in April 1930, he became the first Test batsman to score a triple century, with a knock of 325.

Out before the start

Eddie Barlow was once dismissed in a Test match before the official starting time. The occasion was the third Test between South Africa and Australia in Durban on 20 January 1967. The pitch was well grassed, and Barlow hit the first ball, a half-volley, back to the bowler, Garth McKenzie. Barlow was out caught and bowled for a golden duck. The time was 10.59am – one minute before the official starting time.

Epileptic attack stops play

England captain Tony Greig had a dramatic collapse when making his debut for Eastern Province against Transvaal on 27 November 1970. Greig suffered from epilepsy, but had learnt to control the problem. Shortly before the start of play he felt dizzy, and a doctor advised him not to play. But 25-year-old Greig insisted on taking the field, as this was his first match for Eastern Province, after having played previously for Border. He was playing with the Pollocks – Peter and Graeme – and he wasn't going to give up the opportunity too easily.

The dizziness got worse, but Greig managed to hold on to two catches to get rid of Brian Bath and Peter Carlstein. Then he had an epileptic attack. The Transvaal captain Ali Bacher, a practising doctor, ran onto the field to give Greig an injection. Greig subsequently learnt that Bacher had been warned about Greig's condition by Peter Pollock.

A group of teammates held Greig down until the fit had passed. Somehow, the authorities managed to convince the press and 8,000 spectators at the Wanderers that Greig had suffered from sunstroke. Eastern Province nearly had a double blow that day. Peter Pollock foolishly put his hand in Greig's mouth to release his tongue. During the seizure, Greig very nearly bit off Pollock's bowling finger. He didn't bowl in Transvaal's first innings, nor did he bat in Eastern Province's first innings, but he returned to the fray for the second innings, taking 0 for 39 and scoring 28 runs. Transvaal won the match by 156 runs.

Wherever he hangs his cap ...

Western Province opening batsman Lawrence Seeff had an unusual and very lucky escape while playing against Transvaal at the Wanderers in March 1979. It was the 19-year-old's eighth game for Western Province and his first at the imposing Bullring, where he had to contend with the higher altitude and higher bounce.

He was also up against a formidable Transvaal team, with the bulk of the players in that side going on to become part of the 'Mean Machine' era of Transvaal cricket in the 1980s.

Province needed a near-impossible 383 for victory on the final day, facing a bowling attack that included Rupert Hanley, Doug Neilson, Clive Rice and Alan Kourie. The visitors decided to dig in and bat out the day for a draw.

The young Seeff was doing a great job of frustrating the Transvaal bowlers when a fed-up Hanley, one of the fastest bowlers of his generation, bowled him a bouncer, forcing him to take dramatic evasive action.

Batsmen didn't wear helmets in those days, and Seeff whipped his head out of the way. His cap flew into the air and landed on top of the stumps – without dislodging the bails. The players stared in disbelief as the cap hung on the wicket as if it had been placed on a coat hook.

Umpires Denzil Bezuidenhout and Syd Moore agreed that Seeff was not out and he was allowed to remove the cap ever so carefully and resume his innings. The Transvaal players weren't amused and Seeff batted on for three hours for a plodding 33 runs.

However, his efforts to thwart the Transvaal bowlers were in vain, and Province were eventually all out for 265, giving Transvaal a 127-run victory.

For the chop

In a story that could only happen in South Africa, Lulama Masikazana was picked to keep wicket for Eastern Province against England A on their tour to South Africa in 1993, but had to withdraw from selection. He was due to have his initiation ceremony and be circumcised, and it might have been a little difficult to wear a box and keep with, well, such a wound.

A former South African Schools and Nuffield Week player, Masikazana played first-class and limited-overs cricket for six years, representing Eastern Province in 38 first-class matches and 24 domestic games.

Making his Mark

There have been many spectacular career meltdowns, but you would struggle to find a life that has seen as much trouble as that of Zimbabwean cricketer Mark Vermeulen. It is also the story of one of the most incredible comebacks.

In 2006, Vermeulen was banned from playing cricket in England for trying to strike a spectator with a boundary marker and was then arrested for arson after he burnt down the pavilion at the Zimbabwe Cricket Academy.

He had been forced to leave England after going quite mad during a game there. He had thrown a cricket ball at the crowd, who had been taunting him while playing as the professional for the Lancashire League club, Werneth. When that didn't satisfy him, he picked up a boundary-marker spike and advanced on the spectators, screaming at them, but was tackled to the ground by a club official, who punched him several times on the head. He was banned for ten years, although that was later reduced to three.

He returned to Zimbabwe, but a sense of alienation and rejection from Zimbabwe Cricket after being left out of the 30-man national squad tipped him over the edge yet again. He even tried to force his way into the house of Robert Mugabe, the President of Zimbabwe and the patron of Zimbabwe Cricket, which would have got him shot by trigger-happy guards had they not taken pity on him and sent him on his way. He went to the Harare Sports Club, where the team was training.

'The national squad guys were there training and they had totally discarded me. I'd expected to be in that squad,' he told UK newspaper the *Telegraph*. 'I just thought, "f**k this, I don't want anyone else to have the opportunity to play if they're not willing to give me the opportunity".'

His first attempt at arson, when he tried to burn down the Zimbabwe Cricket Academy headquarters at the Harare Sports Club, was thwarted when someone saw the smoke. Vermeulen went to the Academy the very next night, and this time was successful. Everything inside the building was destroyed; Vermeulen had set fire to the thatch roof. He was arrested, charged with arson and a trial date set. He was facing 25 years in jail, but something in his head told him this was not the end of his cricket career. It would have been the end of a normal person's life, but Vermeulen was not normal.

It could be traced back to January 2004, when Vermeulen, a talented sportsman with a Test century under his belt and who had once been his country's national javelin champion, was hit on the head by Irfan Pathan when playing against India in Brisbane in the VB Series. The ball smashed into his forehead between the grille and the peak, felling him. He had also been hit on the head in the nets a year before.

'I went to pull a rising ball and top-edged it through the gap between the grille and peak of the helmet. I thought I was okay but when I took off the helmet, the fielders could see the indentation in my skull.

'The Australian doctor was shaking as he told me, "This is the riskiest operation you could have." Bone had fractured over my eye and another piece in my sinuses had to be taken out and put back with titanium plates.'

He began batting four months later, but would get angry for no reason and began going off the rails. His form dropped, he lost his fiancée and became moody.

At his trial, it was discovered he had psychiatric problems, including partial complex epilepsy, brought about by the Pathan ball to the head.

'Doctors found my personality was altered by abnormal misfiring in my brain's left hemisphere. The illness causes loss of impulse control and compromises anger-management,' said Vermeulen, who is on medication and goes for regular sessions with a psychiatrist.

He was found not guilty in January 2008, then approached Zimbabwe Cricket and offered to pay back the $150,000 damage he had done to the Academy from match fees if he was allowed to play for his country again. They agreed.

He was picked for the Zimbabwe squad for the ODI series against Bangladesh, and in his first international match in five years scored 92 at the Queen's Sports Club in Bulawayo as an opener. It was not enough to stop Bangladesh from winning by eight wickets with 93 balls remaining, but it did add another chapter to one of the more remarkable returns by any sportsman.

He was warned by the Australian surgeon who patched him together in Brisbane that if he got hit on the head again he might die, but that seems to be a risk he is willing to take: 'Every time I walk out to bat could be my last, but I don't really worry too much about that. I love cricket too much. Everyone on this planet experiences their own journey through life and I've certainly had a pretty eventful one and hopefully now I'll have a quiet end to my career.'

HUMOROUS STORIES

Get him to the wedding on time

When South African fast bowler André Nel and his fiancée Deanne set a wedding date of 17 January 2004, they had no idea that Nel's subsequent form would make him an indispensable member of the South African team to play in the fourth Test against the West Indies at Centurion that month. With the wedding guests having accepted their invitations, the church booked, the reception organised and Nel selected for the South African team, the big fast bowler was faced with a choice – to attend his wedding or play cricket. So he did both. He played on the first two days, and then made sure he got to the church on time by taking a helicopter. Bad light worked in his favour, as play finished slightly early on day two, and Nel got married an hour after the close of play. The following day he had an early start to his honeymoon and dismissed the great Brian Lara twice in the same day as the West Indies followed on. If asked what was more special – getting married or dismissing Lara twice in the same match on the same day – Nel would probably be stumped for an answer.

Get him to the match on time

There are only five reported cases of a batsman being dismissed 'timed out' in a first-class match, and making the list as only the second person to suffer this unusual dismissal is Eastern Province's Andrew Jordaan. Playing a Howa Bowl match against Transvaal in

Port Elizabeth in the 1987/88 season, Jordaan had been not out overnight. During the night, a torrential rainstorm had left many roads impassable, and Jordaan wasn't able to get to the ground in time to resume his innings. The umpires timed him out after waiting the requisite two minutes on appeal from the Transvaal team. The law has since been changed to allow a batsman three minutes to get onto the field.

One of the other four incidents of a batsman being timed out also occurred in South Africa, but affected the West Indian import Vasbert Drakes. Drakes was given out playing for Border against Free State at Buffalo Park in East London on 27 September 2002. Drakes could be forgiven for being late – he wasn't even at the ground when he was due to bat. He had been delayed in Colombo, trying to fly out of Sri Lanka with the West Indian team at the end of a tour. He managed to get to East London in time to bowl in Free State's first innings and took 2 for 45, before scoring seven runs in Border's second innings as his team slumped to an innings and 41-run defeat.

Mbeki wins for Sussex

Politicians are known to interfere in sporting events for different reasons. Two young South African students living in Brighton, who went on to become prominent politicians, were responsible for the great West Indian team that toured England in 1966 suffering a loss against Sussex.

Thabo Mbeki was a postgraduate student at Sussex University when he and fellow students, including Essop Pahad who would later become Minister in the Presidency, threw a party for the West Indian cricketers who had just thrashed England in the first Test at Old Trafford by an innings and 40 runs. The team was playing a county fixture against Sussex at the County Ground, Hove, on 11 June 1966. The liquor flowed and the party became so rowdy that the police were called. However, the police quickly realised that the revellers were their local team's opposition in a match that was on the go, apologised for the inconvenience and wisely allowed the festivities to continue.

The next day, the badly hungover West Indians carried on their match. Batting in their second innings, they were 62 runs in arrears. They struggled to 67 all out, with captain Garry Sobers, who failed to live up to his surname, managing just eight runs. They eventually lost by nine wickets and Sussex became the first county side to beat the powerful team within two days. The West Indies went on to win the Test series 3-1 with one Test drawn.

Fried calamari stops play

Play was halted for ten minutes during a Castle Cup match between Boland and Border at the Paarl Cricket Club Ground in Paarl in February 1995. Chasing 121 for victory, and going well, Border batsman Daryll Cullinan hit a ball from Boland's Roger Telemachus for a six into the crowd sitting on one of the grass embankments. The ball landed up in a frying pan of calamari.

The *Wisden* report described the moment as 'fried calamari stops play'. The report went to say: 'It was about ten minutes before the ball was cool enough for the umpires to remove the grease. Even then, Telemachus was unable to grip the ball and it had to be replaced.'

When play finally resumed, Cullinan steered his team to an easy nine-wicket victory.

Porn stops play

Legendary BBC commentator Brian Johnston was a great one for practical jokes. During the fifth Test between England and South Africa at the Oval in August 1960, Johnston decided to liven up proceedings, with the needle having gone out of the series after England had won the first three. Johnston stuffed what he called 'a rather rude photograph' into an envelope and got South Africa's 12th man, Charlie Griffin, to take it out to Neil Adcock on the field.

As Johnston recounted: 'Adcock stuffed it into his trouser pocket until he had bowled another over. He then opened the envelope, saw the photograph and began to roar with laughter. He signalled the rest of his team to come and have a look; and even the two umpires, Charlie Elliott and Eddie Phillipson, could not resist taking a peep. Soon everyone on the field was laughing and all we could say on TV was that Adcock had obviously had some very good news from home.'

Drink all night, bat all day

Hylton Ackerman was in trouble. He'd spent the night drinking before a game and Eddie Barlow, his Western Province captain and good friend, wanted to send 'Dutchman' back home on the very next plane.

To ensure that this did not happen, Ackerman simply kept batting. Before Ackerman became captain in 1977/78, Province was captained by Barlow, who insisted that his team were fit and would often take them out on runs. Ackerman once went out for a 'liquid dinner' when Western Province was playing Eastern Province in Port Elizabeth. He missed the team bus the next morning and caught a taxi to the ground, arriving late, and was informed that as soon as he lost his wicket, he would be on the next plane home to Cape Town. So he did what every good batsman/drinker would do, and stayed at the wicket all day, scoring an undefeated 141.

As mentioned, Barlow liked his team to be fit and they had to go on long runs and endure hectic training sessions. The Province wicketkeeper Gavin Pfuhl arrived one evening with a note from his doctor saying that he had 'heart problems' and should try to avoid any physical exertion. Pfuhl headed for home, but, said Barlow, 'something just didn't seem right'. So 'Bunter' led the team on their jog to Pfuhl's house in Newlands, ran through his rose bushes and into the lounge, where they found him sipping on a beer.

'We formed a circle around him and watched him work through his physical jerks,' said Barlow.

Pack light

Eddie Barlow's Province teammates definitely liked to prank one another. Before a trip to Johannesburg Province batsman Gerald Innes told the team's off-spinner Harry Bromfield that because Johannesburg was a long way away and 'uphill all the way', the jet could not take much luggage, and so all the players had been asked to travel as light as possible. The next day Bromfield arrived at the airport with a tiny suitcase, much to the amusement of his teammates.

The fastest of the slowest

The second Test between South Africa and the West Indies in June 2010 was a fractious affair, with clashes between Dale Steyn and Sulieman Benn, and Jacques Kallis and Kemar Roach. South Africa won the Test and wrapped up the series, but did not start celebrating properly until another serious clash was settled. It seems there was an ongoing argument between Graeme Smith and Paul Harris as to just who was the quicker sprinter.

Stuart Hess of *The Star*, one of the few South African journalists to witness this, said it was quite a sight to behold.

> Immediately after the presentation, and my interview with him, there was Biff [Graeme Smith] on the ground doing stretches, with help from AB [de Villiers]. Harry [Paul Harris] stripped

down to his cycling shorts and decides it would be better to go barefoot. I'm in the middle of an interview with Botha at the time, and I can see this oke is not interested in talking to me, so we all stop. This is one thing you want to see. There was a false start, I think that was Harry's fault. Someone had unravelled a roll of toilet paper to use as the finishing line. Biff triumphs, but it was a close one as Harry held him until the last 20 metres. Biff charged upstairs after winning, arms aloft, before striking a Usain Bolt pose at the top of the stairs leading into the dressing room.

The team celebrated heartily, reported Hess, and were still in the changing room two hours after the formalities and the 100-metre sprint.

A fines time indeed

The celebrations of the South Africans after they had wrapped up the Test series against Australia at the Melbourne Cricket Ground in December 2008 were something to behold. Having beaten the Baggy Greens convincingly by nine wickets, the South Africans were subdued as they walked out on the field and impressed the Australian commentators on Channel 9 with their graciousness in thanking their hosts for the game. Graeme Smith says he remembers cases and cases of beer and champagne being delivered to their dressing room, Brett Lee and Shane Watson coming across for a beer, and the wives, girlfriends and children of the players and management all joining in.

Then, however, the proper celebrating began. 'A cricket fines meeting is no place for ladies or children,' said Smith. The fines meeting was led by Neil McKenzie and Mark Boucher, who were the usual suspects in charge of anything involving beer or humour. Loads of 'down-downs' were had and the fines lasted a long, long time. After the fines, the players decided to head down to the field for a little bit of fun and to revisit the pitch where they had won the biggest Test series of their lives four hours earlier. The Australian security guards were not best pleased with them, nor with Paul Harris, who was puffing on a huge cigar. The MCG is a non-smoking venue, so he was ordered to put it out.

Smith, giddy on, er, life, and a few beers, chased the seagulls around for five minutes, as you do, before they all gathered on the pitch and sang the team song. They also turned to the Australian changing room, long since deserted, and began to belt out the old English football song: 'You're not singing any more.' This was a reference to the Australian team always reciting 'Under the Southern Cross I stand' whenever they win a match. If you are a South African journalist, you will have heard that sung a lot, once in the twilight at the Wanderers with the ground empty.

A light caught Smith's eye. The lights were still on in the press box. 'Oh dear, we'd just given them quite a show,' said Smith. The singalong was mentioned in the papers the next day. 'Thankfully with plenty of good humour and understanding. They knew how proud we were. And no harm was done.'

Stuart Hess of *The Star*, who was sitting in that press box, said every single one of the journalists laughed and applauded the team for singing. They had gained the respect of the toughest cricketing country in the world.

The underpants brigade

The South African team that toured England in 1965 also walked to the middle of the field to celebrate after they had won the second Test at Trent Bridge. Graeme Pollock's 125 had swung the match in South Africa's favour and they won by 94 runs. Like the South Africans of 2008, Eddie Barlow, the two Pollocks and the rest wandered out to the pitch, some of them dressed only in their underpants and, naturally, armed with beers. 'We proceeded to underline our success by watering the wicket, just as we had pissed on the English during the match,' said Barlow. 'It wasn't classy, but someone took a photograph, which was published in the newspapers back home, and most people loved it.'

Peter Pollock had said before the Trent Bridge Test match that if South Africa won, he would swear to stay off alcohol. He took 10 for 87 from his 48 overs and, true to his word, did not touch a drop of booze. For two hours. 'He did abstain from a celebratory drink, at least until he had decided the Lord would be happy with two hours of penance, whereupon he happily drank a bottle of beer. He had earned every drop.'

South Africa drew the third Test and won the series, only the second by a South African team in England. It never became known as the 'underpants win', though.

Quick runs for lots of runs

AB de Villiers's tenth Test century was brought up in the fourth ball of the 132nd over of the second Test between the West Indies and South Africa in June 2010.

It was noticeable that he sped up his batting considerably in the final two overs as he approached his ton, a pained expression on his face. On 89, he belted Sulieman Benn for 12 runs in four balls, including a four and a six, before dashing off the field. He'd needed the toilet quite badly for ages, but didn't want to leave the field before he had his ton. As he ran off, umpires Simon Taufel and Asad Rauf were laughing their heads off when he informed them of his predicament. After the day's play, when he had scored 135, De Villiers said:

> It's happened to me before in Zimbabwe. I don't know how to describe it; it's just one of those feelings that comes to you and there's not much you can do about it – you've got to run off the field. I told Bouchy and that's why I actually went to my hundred quite quickly, I decided to have a go and when I got to the hundred, I told Boucher, 'Jis, I'm going to have to do something here'. I don't know if it's something I ate, but you know when you get that cold sweat on the forehead and when that happened I knew I had to go.

As De Villiers ran out of the dressing room, one of his teammates shouted at him, he turned and smiled as a roll of toilet paper was thrown at him.

Gary 'Cruise' Kirsten

What goes on tour usually stays on tour is an old saying, but then one should make sure that one does not try to chat up the opposition's wives and girlfriends.

On the 1993/94 tour of Australia, when he was still single and innocent, Gary Kirsten spied a bunch of pretty Australian girls and thought he might do them a favour by introducing himself to them and, if possible, chat them up.

After having his attempts rebuffed by said damsels, Kirsten was horrified to discover that he had been trying to chat up the wives and girlfriends of the Australian players. He joked he could not sleep the night before playing the Australians next for he was certain he was going to cop a lot of abuse from them. And sure enough, the next day, the Australians gave it to him by the truckload and nicknamed him Tom Cruise for attempting to be so smooth.

Who's speaking?

When cellphones first came out, Allan Lamb, the South African who captained England, got one, and during a county match at Northampton, walked to the middle, reached into his pocket, pulled out the phone and asked umpire Dickie Bird to hold on to it while he batted. 'Meant to leave this in the dressing room. Look after it for me, Dickie.'

Bird was taken aback, but took the phone, which rang five

minutes later. Lamb, who was standing at the other end, shouted across at Bird: 'Answer it, Dickie, and tell them to ring back.' Bird did so. On the other end was Ian Botham. 'What's the score?' asked Botham. Bird's actual reply was unrecorded, but it is safe to say he spluttered and went a bright shade of red.

Sir Ian told another story of when the two were playing together for England, and though we quote it word for word, we reckon he may be exaggerating a tad. Still, it's too good a story to leave out:

> Back when cellphones had just started, Lamby was backing a horse at Ascot. We were playing Pakistan, and Lamby had to go in just as the race started. So I gave him my phone, told him I'd message with the result. He walks out and gives it to Dickie, says, 'Take a message if it rings.' So I send the message just as Waqar [Younis] is steaming in, knowing it would reach a moment before he jumps. Well, it reaches Dickie – who's never seen a cellphone before – at the perfect moment. So you have Dickie jumping like a lunatic, Waqar, hit slap bang on his neck by a flailing arm, Lamby looking for a hole to jump into and the balcony bobbing up and down with the weight of the entire England team rolling around.

The Kotie Award

The Kotie Award is named after Professor Kotie Grove, the respected and much-loved Afrikaans commentator. It's an award – although no trophy exists – given to the commentator who manages, accidentally or through sheer silliness, to make the biggest mistake during a commentary shift.

It was instituted by Mike Haysman, the Australian commentator, when he was at SuperSport before he left for the US. Kotie was the inaugural winner of the award after he had managed to have a very rude Afrikaans word flashed across the country's TV screens. Kotie had been attempting to show fellow commentator Hylton Ackerman how to use the telestrator during a break in play and wrote said rude word on it, which begins with 'P'. When they came back from lunch, Kotie switched on the telestrator. Unfortunately, the word was still on it and Ackerman dived to the screen and started trying to wipe the four-letter word off with his hand. The plug was pulled out, but it was too late. 'Sitting at home, the entire Grove family were watching the game on television,' said Grove. 'My son turned to my wife and said: "Ma, that's Dad's handwriting!"'

Ackerman, bizarrely enough, was the next recipient of the Kotie Award after he managed to mangle his words and said of a difficult wicket: 'You can't play c**ts and hookers on a pitch like this.'

Gerald de Kock, one of the country's best and most versatile commentators, would have won the award, but his biggest faux pas came years before the award was instituted. During the broadcast of the opening ceremony of the 1999 All African Games in Johannesburg, De Kock gushed: 'I don't care what c*** you go to, you won't see a better ceremony than that.' He also managed to annoy one bank and please another when, in the action of handing over a bottle of champagne to Shaun Pollock, who had been man of the match in a Standard Bank-sponsored match, he said: 'Here's a bottle of Nedbank bubbly.' Of course, it was Nederburg.

He's bigger than you

Andrew Symonds is not the first Australian to get into trouble after drinking at a Cape Town night club, but one night he almost picked on someone he might have regretted picking on. After a few sharpies in March 2006, Symonds decided that he didn't like the way a big fellow was looking at him and decided the two should 'go outside to sort it out'.

Unfortunately, the big fellow was an unidentified member of the Cheetahs Super 14 team, down in Cape Town to play the Stormers. Fortunately, Michael Clarke calmed things down.

'I was on my way out of the VIP area when Pup [Michael Clarke] zoomed in to steer me away and calm things down,' said Symonds in his book, *Roy: Going for Broke*. 'Big Ollie [the prop Ollie le Roux] did his bit to keep everyone happy too. I owe Pup big time. Looking back, I realise now I was headed for the sort of strife that could have brought a swift end to my tour and possibly my international career. It was a sobering reminder that old-school ways where two men sort out their difference one-on-one are long gone.'

Especially if they are rather large fellows who take physical contact for a living.

Night owl

Before South Africa played Australia in Durban in March 2006, AB De Villiers, who was opening the batting the next day, wanted to get plenty of sleep. He went to bed at 8pm, but after a fitful sleep he woke up in a panic, as his alarm clock showed it was 10.30.

The Test was scheduled to start at 10am and he realised he was late for the second day. He quickly showered, ran to the dining room where they were clearing away the food and grabbed a slice of bread. He ran to the foyer to get a taxi to Kingsmead, only to see it was dark outside. It was 10.30pm and he had slept for only two hours. He tried to sneak back to his room, but was caught by teammates, who forced the story out of him.

POLITICS, PROTESTS AND APARTHEID

White cricket's first anti-apartheid protest

Cricketers aren't normally known for their overt political activism, but an extraordinary act of defiance against the apartheid policies of the South African government came on 3 April 1971 during a match between Currie Cup champions Transvaal and a Rest of South Africa XI at Newlands in Cape Town. The South African Cricket Association President, Jack Cheetham, had told the government that SACA would ask the non-racial South African Cricket Board to nominate two players for the end-of-year tour of Australia. Sports Minister Frank Waring angrily rejected the idea. The players, realising their future in international cricket was in serious jeopardy, decided to voice their objection to the government's move in a public show of protest. The Newlands match was part of the Republic Festival, but also served as a final trial before the team to tour Australia would be announced. After consulting with commentator Charles Fortune, a man whose opinion was highly regarded among the players, the teams decided against an outright boycott of the match and opted for a walk-off instead.

Mike Procter bowled the first ball to Barry Richards, who was a guest player for Transvaal, which he nudged away for a single; and then the players walked off the field. There was confusion among the spectators, which included four cabinet ministers. Don Mackay-Coghill, who was captaining Transvaal in the absence of Ali Bacher, then read out a statement in the press box: 'We cricketers feel that the time has come for an expression of our views. We fully support the South African Cricket Association's application to include non-whites on the tour of Australia if good enough and, furthermore, subscribe to merit being the only criterion on the cricket field.'

The players then returned to the field and the match continued. Waring was apoplectic with rage and described the walk-off as 'a political demonstration designed for overseas consumption'. The protest was in vain; the South African government refused to budge on its racial policies, and the tour to Australia was ultimately cancelled.

When the touring team was announced after the Newlands match, Mackay-Coghill was not included in the team. Selector Eric Rowan saw him as one of the ringleaders of the protest and after he had read out the statement in the press box, Mackay-Coghill was confronted by an angry Rowan, who told him, 'That's it; you've just done your dash!'

Rowan was a well-known National Party supporter, even though he didn't often show cabinet ministers the respect they might have expected. When FW de Klerk was Minister of Sport in 1978/79, he was introduced to Rowan by Transvaal Cricket Union chairman Joe Pamensky. Rowan swaggered over, looked De Klerk up and down, and said: 'I hope you've got more f*cking brains than hair.'

An infamous 'V' sign

Eric Rowan was fond of courting controversy. In the first Test against England at Ellis Park in December 1948, Rowan had scored just eight runs in the first innings. As he walked out in South Africa's follow-on second innings, needing a solid knock to save the game, the team to play in the second Test at Newlands was announced. Rowan wasn't in it. He was furious. He discarded his gloves and his box (something he often did, but not in Test matches), and hit 156 not out in just over six hours to draw the match. To ensure that his protest of batting without gloves and a box hadn't been missed by the selectors, he also flashed them a two-fingered salute. Rowan was challenged about the insult, and he claimed he was giving a Churchillian 'V' for victory. When it was pointed out that he had made the sign the wrong way round, *Wisden* reports that he replied: 'That depends on what part of the ground you're sitting [in].'

Rowan might have been angry about the political protest at Newlands in 1971, but he was not above public protest himself. He was involved in a controversial protest during South Africa's county match against Lancashire at Old Trafford on 16 June 1951. The crowd started to boo and slow-handclap him and his batting partner Johnny Waite as they put on 164 for the first wicket. While Waite was irritated, the noise didn't affect Rowan too much. As he put it, 'I always played better to music and I was enjoying baiting them.'

The two of them decided to stage a sit-down protest on the wicket until the noise had subsided. As Rowan walked back to the dressing room after making 66, he had an altercation with a spectator who questioned his parentage. Typically, Rowan had a caustic response: 'Kiss my Royal Australian!' A reporter on the *Manchester Guardian* overheard Rowan venting about the crowd behaviour, and reported his comments in full, which appeared in the next morning's edition of the newspaper. When Rowan saw the reporter again at Old Trafford, he belted him, and found he was all over the newspaper for a second day running.

He made 277 not out for Transvaal against Griqualand West in 1950/51, then the highest Currie Cup score, and scored 176 before lunch against Rhodesia. He averaged 109 that season. In his 26 Tests he scored 1,965 runs and averaged 43.66; he scored 11,710 first-class runs at 48.58, including 30 centuries. He played for Jeppe Old Boys until he was 51.

Multiracial cricket in the apartheid era

The unlikely venue of Natalspruit staged a famous racially charged cricket match in April 1961 between AS Haque's Transvaal 'non-white' XI and a Johnny Waite XI. Waite's XI included four Springboks and six Currie Cup players.

Haque's XI batted first and Armien Variawa scored 107 of his team's tally of 207 – a remarkable 51% of the total. A 16-year-old bowler, Tiffie Barnes, took 3 for 35 as Waite's XI were all out for 154.

Haque's XI were undone in their second innings by Mike Macaulay (6 for 40) and Jackie Botten (3 for 17), and collapsed to 75 all out, giving Waite's XI a seemingly easy target of 129 for victory. Whereas a 16-year-old had done much to skittle Waite's XI in the first innings, a 50-year-old did all the damage in the second. Medium-pacer Samson Ntshekisa took 5 for 27 to reduce the opposition to 108 all out, and guide his team to a famous 20-run victory. In one eight-ball over, he took the wickets of Waite, Ken Walter and Sid O'Linn.

Dolly's exile

The first tour of South Africa by a West Indian team was in November 1998, led by the great Brian Lara. But the legendary Frank Worrell nearly led a West Indian tour to South Africa in 1959, organised by the South African Cricket Board of Control (SACBOC). The tour was called off when anti-apartheid organisations in South Africa argued that the tour would condone the ruling National Party's racial policies.

The cancellation of the tour prompted Basil D'Oliveira to further his career in England, with the help of cricket commentator John Arlott. Arlott persuaded the Central Lancashire League club of Middleton to give D'Oliveira a two-year contract in 1960. He scored a thousand runs, took 70 wickets and finished above the great Garry Sobers in the batting averages. By 1964, he was playing county cricket for Worcestershire and made his debut for

England against the West Indies at Lord's in June 1966. He played 44 Tests for England, scoring 2,484 runs, including five centuries and a top score of 158, at an average of 40. He also took 47 wickets at an average of 39.55.

When the England team was to be selected to tour South Africa in December 1968, D'Oliveira had established himself as an all-rounder, having played 16 Tests with a batting average of 48.60. He was also one of *Wisden's* Cricketers of the Year for 1967.

South Africa's Minister of the Interior, Pieter le Roux, warned that D'Oliveira would not be allowed into South Africa if he was selected, a warning repeated by Prime Minister John Vorster. Vorster even secretly discussed giving D'Oliveira a bribe not to come if selected.

D'Oliveira made it difficult to ignore him by scoring a career-best 158 in the fifth Test against Australia at the Oval in August 1968. The selectors met until 2am, with the minutes of the meeting strangely going missing, and opted to leave D'Oliveira out of the 16-man squad. Tom Cartwright was selected, but 20 days later he pulled out after failing to recover from a shoulder injury. He was replaced by D'Oliveira. Vorster was furious, saying: 'We are not prepared to receive a team thrust upon us by people whose interests are not in the game but to gain certain political objectives which they do not even attempt to hide. The MCC team is not the team of the MCC but of the anti-apartheid movement.'

A week later, on 24 September 1968, the MCC called off the tour. The next time an England team visited South Africa was in December 1995, led by Mike Atherton.

When D'Oliveira's Test career ended in August 1972, he returned to South Africa the following month and was brought to

Port Elizabeth by a sponsorship from the South African Bottling Company, and, according to André Odendaal's *The Story of an African Game*, he created a whole new dimension in the local game. He promptly broke a SACBOC batting record with 182 for Eastern Province against Transvaal. That record was broken two years later by another big-name player, West Indian Rohan Kanhai, who played for Transvaal in the 1974/75 season. His 188 not out against Eastern Province set the new Board record.

D'Oliveira played two seasons for Eastern Province before returning to England where he retired from first-class cricket in 1980.

John Thicknesse, writing for Cricinfo, made a pertinent comment about D'Oliveira: 'When you watched Dolly flaying the opposition's bowlers with meaty back-foot clumps, or frustrating their batsmen with outward-drifting medium pace of cloying accuracy (his economy rate in Tests was 1.95 runs per over) there was one sharp regret … if only he'd been spotted at 19 rather than 29. Then D'Oliveira would have put the runs and wickets in the book that would have shown future generations what he unmistakably was – one of cricket's greats.'

The boycott that had nothing to do with apartheid

If South Africa's first ODI and first World Cup matches after isolation were dramatic, it seems almost inevitable that the country's first Test match after isolation should produce its fair share of stories.

Prior to exclusion from international cricket by the ICC, South Africa's touring teams became increasingly subjected to anti-apartheid protests in the late 1960s. It seems extraordinary then that, after the demise of apartheid, South Africa should play its first Test match in the midst of a boycott.

This time, though, apartheid had nothing to do with the stayaway. The match was against the West Indies at the Kensington Oval in Bridgetown, Barbados on 18 April 1992. A local Barbadian player, Anderson Cummins, had not been selected and had been replaced by Kenny Benjamin from Antigua. The local fans were outraged and decided to boycott the Test.

In front of near-empty stands, the West Indies and South Africa played a memorable match. South Africa needed just 79 runs for victory on the final day with eight wickets standing, but the pace of Curtly Ambrose and Courtney Walsh, bowling unchanged through the morning, ripped through the South African team on a deteriorating wicket, and South Africa managed only 26 more runs before being bowled out, to lose the match by 52 runs.

That devastating bowling performance by Ambrose and Walsh tends to overshadow a few more remarkable statistics from that return to Test cricket for South Africa. Ten members of the South African team made their Test debuts. The only South African who had previously played Test cricket was captain Kepler Wessels, who had played 24 Tests for Australia.

Richard Snell took 8 for 157 – four wickets in each innings. Andrew Hudson made a century on debut – 163, almost emulating

Wessels on his debut for Australia (against England in Brisbane when he scored 162).

Politics and sport collide

A cricket match played at the Jabavu Stadium in Moroka, Soweto, in October 1973 was a politically charged affair. The Derrick Robins XI (named after an English businessman with a passion for cricket and a desire to break South Africa's sporting isolation) played against the South African XI, made up of local black cricketers. It was the first time an overseas touring team was made up of players of different races, and the first time an overseas touring team played in Soweto. The touring side included Pakistan's Younis Ahmed, and the West Indies' John Shepherd.

The match was described in white sports circles as a breakthrough, but this was rejected by the South African Cricket Board of Control, which argued that the match maintained the racial status quo, as whites and blacks were still not allowed to play in the same team in domestic cricket competitions.

For the record, the tourists won the match by 222 runs. For many white cricket writers, this was their first glimpse of the prodigiously talented Khaya Majola, who was described in one article as 'a natural and talented cricketer'. Majola would go on to become one of the key figures in the creation of the United Cricket Board on 29 June 1991.

Tears of joy

One of the iconic photographs of the first years after South Africa's return from isolation is of Steve Tshwete, the ANC's go-to guy on sport, hugging a shy-looking but broadly smiling Kepler Wessels after South Africa had beaten Australia in their opening match of the Cricket World Cup in Australia in 1992.

Wessels, the captain, had scored 81 not out as South Africa beat Australia by nine wickets with 13 balls remaining. Tshwete, who was an emotional chap and had spent time on Robben Island, had gone down to the dressing room and headed towards Wessels and Peter Kirsten, who played for Border, the traditional black stronghold of South African cricket. He had tears streaming down his cheeks and clasped Kirsten's head to his chest: 'Peter, you've saved the country.' Just in case Kirsten hadn't realised this, faxes from Nelson Mandela and FW de Klerk followed saying the same thing.

Tshwete even took the time to hug Mike Gatting, the former England captain, who had led the last and ill-fated rebel tour to South Africa, which was curtailed after pressure from protesters.

There was a sour moment for Kirsten when Peter van der Merwe, the convener of selectors, walked past him and said, 'The selectors got it right after all.' Kirsten later learnt that Van der Merwe had not wanted to pick him, but had wanted wicketkeeper Dave Richardson to play at three instead of him.

Hooray for Henry!

The realities of apartheid in the 1970s were brought home to Eddie Barlow and the rest of the Western Province team when, on a bus trip home after an away match, they decided to stop at a pub in Somerset West for a drink.

Omar Henry, who would go on to represent South Africa and become a national selector, was coloured and as he walked in with his teammates, the bartender stopped them and said, 'Hey! He can't come in.'

Barlow argued with the man, and was told: 'Just call this number in Pretoria. It's a 24-hour number and you should be able to get special dispensation for your friend to have a beer in here as well.'

Barlow called; special dispensation was granted. It was a process they had to go through just about every time they wanted to have a drink with Henry. On one occasion, when Henry was refused admission to a steakhouse, the entire team walked out in protest and vowed never to return.

Barlow became involved in politics later in his career, joined the Progressive Federal Party and was asked by Frederik van Zyl Slabbert to stand as a candidate in a by-election for the vacant Simonstown seat. He lost, with one wag suggesting that PFP stood for Played For Province.

Barlow also started the South African Sports Office in London in 1984, the aim of which was to encourage change in South Africa through participation in sport and encourage non-racialism in sport. In this, he was up against Sam Ramsamy's South African Non-Racial Olympic Committee, whose policy was 'no normal sport in an abnormal society'.

It was an ill-judged move by Barlow. He received a fair amount of publicity, but little support from international bodies or the South African government of the time.

Too fast, too coloured

Armien 'Krom' Hendricks should have been South Africa's first cricketing superstar, but racism and segregation stopped him from being allowed to tour with the first South African team to England in 1894.

Hendricks was a Malay born in the Cape, and was regarded as the fastest bowler in the country at the time. On the England tour to South Africa in 1891/92, Hendricks had impressed the English when they played a Malay invitation team in Cape Town. Hendricks took four wickets for 50 runs, batted at six and scored 8 and 5. Walter Read, the England captain, told his South African counterparts: 'If you send a team to England, send Hendricks; he will be a drawcard and is to my mind the Spofforth [Frederick Spofforth, the Australian bowler] of South Africa.'

Spofforth, known as the 'demon', was Australia's first truly fast bowler to terrorise England teams. The England batsman George Hearne agreed: 'A Malay named Hendricks was very fast indeed. In our last match against the Malays the wicket was very bad and we didn't like facing the man at all. I was captain during the match and everyone began to ask me to let someone else go in his place.

The ball flew over our heads in all directions.'

The South African authorities listened and his name was among those nominated to the selectors for the tour. However, a storm was brewing off the field.

The Transvaal newspaper *The Star* came to the fore and advocated that he be included in the team, but this did not sit well in Cape Town. The *Cape Times* suggested he be taken as a 'baggage man' so that there 'could be absolutely no objection to Hendricks on account of his being a Malay'. Except that Hendricks objected most vehemently, saying he was insulted. He also wrote a letter to the paper in which he said that he was, in fact, not a Malay, but a Christian with a father 'born of Dutch parents' and a mother from St Helena.

Racism reared its ugly head with South African batsman Bernard Tancred suggesting that after his 'impudent letter, I should certainly leave him out. If he wants to go on the same footing as the others, I would not have him at any price. As baggage man they might take him and play him in one or two of the matches when the conditions suited him. To take him as an equal would from a South African point of view be impolitic, not to say intolerable . . .'

A reader of *The Star* said that if South Africa were going to travel to England and be beaten, then they should 'at least take a licking like white men ... it is imperative that the line be drawn sharp, straight and unbroken between white and coloured'.

HG Cadwallader, the secretary of the South African Cricket Association, pushed for Hendricks's inclusion and wrote a letter to the newspapers saying so, but the president of the Western Province Cricket Union, Sir William Milton, consulted with the

Prime Minister of the Cape Colony, Cecil Rhodes, and vetoed his selection.

Milton, who was close to Rhodes and later became the Secretary for Native Affairs and Administrator of Southern Rhodesia, was angry with Cadwallader and engineered that he should not be considered as manager of the England team to tour in 1894. Cadwallader still toured with England, but as a journalist, and took every chance he could to write of how England were getting a pasting and how they had made a mistake in not picking Hendricks.

The fast bowler was also prevented from playing England on the 1895/96 tour and was dropped by Western Province as Milton wielded his influence.

OTHER TRIVIA,
FACTS AND FIGURES

Wins around the cricketing world

Mark Boucher and Shaun Pollock are the only cricketers to have been on winning South African sides against every Test country – home and away. They have been members of winning teams which beat Australia, New Zealand, England, India, Pakistan, Sri Lanka, the West Indies and Bangladesh both at home and away. Makhaya Ntini falls one short of a full house, having never beaten Sri Lanka away.

The double-bounce dismissal

AB de Villiers is believed to be the only South African batsman in the post-isolation era to have lost his wicket in a Test match to a ball that bounced twice. In South Africa's first innings against Bangladesh in Mirpur in February 2008, De Villiers was caught and bowled by Mohammad Ashraful. The ball bounced twice, and, thinking it was a no-ball, De Villiers took a swipe. Law 24 states that a delivery is illegal if the ball bounces *more than twice*, making Ashraful's delivery quite legal.

De Villiers also holds the record for the most Test innings without scoring a duck. He avoided the ignominy for an extraordinary 78 Test innings in a row, until the second Test against Bangladesh in Centurion in November 2008, when he was stumped by Mushfiqur Rahim off Shakib Al Hasan's bowling for nought in his 79th Test innings. He had broken the previous record, held by Sri Lanka's

Aravinda de Silva, who avoided the dreaded duck for 75 Test innings.

That Test match against Bangladesh also established a remarkable record of ducks, with five batsmen failing to get off the mark in South Africa's innings of 429. It remains the highest Test total to include five noughts. The other non-performers (apart from AB) were Neil McKenzie, Morné Morkel, Mondi Zondeki and Makhaya Ntini. Scores of 162 from Ashwell Prince, 117 from Mark Boucher and 71 from Hashim Amla ensured South Africa would win by an innings and 48 runs. South Africa held the previous record of 390 runs in an innings that included five ducks against England at the Old Wanderers in December 1938.

Tons for two countries

Kepler Wessels is the only cricketer to have scored Test centuries for two different countries – Australia and South Africa. He scored 162 for Australia in his Test debut against England in Brisbane on 26 November 1982. When South Africa played its first Test match on home soil after readmission to the ICC, against India in Durban on 13 November 1992, Wessels scored 118 to achieve the rare double.

He was just ten runs short of achieving the double in ODI cricket, scoring his only ODI century of 107 for Australia, but managing just 90 for South Africa.

Double opening ducks

The rare sight of two openers in one side each scoring a duck in a Test match was made even more extraordinary in South Africa's Test match against Sri Lanka in Kandy in August 2000, when both openers for both sides failed to get off the mark. In South Africa's first innings, Gary Kirsten was trapped LBW for a duck on the fifth ball of the match, and was followed six balls later by Neil McKenzie when he was caught without scoring. In Sri Lanka's second innings, both Marvan Atapattu and Sanath Jayasuriya were out LBW without scoring. South Africa won the match by just seven runs.

One Test, two tons

Five South African batsmen have scored centuries in both innings of a Test match. Alan Melville got 189 and 104 against England in the first Test in Nottingham in June 1947. Bruce Mitchell got 120 and 189 against England in the fifth Test of the same series at the Oval in August 1947. However, 49 years would pass before Gary Kirsten achieved the same feat, this time against India in the second Test in Calcutta in November 1996, scoring 146 and 133. Jacques Kallis weighed in with two tons in a Test – 155 and 100 not out against Pakistan in Karachi in October 2007. Hashim Amla's 114 and 123 not out against India in Kolkata in February 2010 completes the South African list.

Melville's tons were part of a series of four centuries in succession in Test matches – a feat never before achieved by a South African Test player. But what was more remarkable about this achievement is that eight years and three months (which included World War II) separated his first and second centuries. Melville scored 103 in South Africa's second innings of the famous drawn Timeless Test at Kingsmead in March 1939. That was South Africa's last Test match before the outbreak of World War II. South Africa's first post-war Test match was in June 1947 against England at Trent Bridge in Nottingham, where Melville scored 189 and 104 in the drawn Test. He scored 117 in the second Test at Lord's for his fourth successive ton.

A tiring Test time

Two South African Test players have spent the entire match on the field: Jackie McGlew and Herschelle Gibbs. In South Africa's victory against New Zealand at the Basin Reserve in Wellington in the first Test in March 1953, McGlew opened the batting, scoring 255 not out in almost nine hours. He carried his bat in South Africa's innings of 524 for 8 declared, and then fielded throughout the New Zealand first and second innings following on, as South Africa won by an innings and 180 runs.

Gibbs was on the field for the duration of the rain-interrupted second Test against New Zealand in Christchurch in 2000. He fielded in New Zealand's first innings, and then scored 211 not out – his maiden Test century – in almost 11 hours as South Africa scored 442 for 1. Gibbs was back on the field for New Zealand's second innings on the fifth day as the match fizzled out into a draw.

A short World Cup ODI

Boland Park in Paarl hosted the shortest ever World Cup ODI, and the second shortest ODI in history, when the match was all over in 143 balls. Sri Lanka beat Canada in a Pool B clash of the 2003 World Cup on 19 February. Sri Lanka rolled Canada out for 36 in 115 balls, and then needed just 28 balls to reach the winning target. At the time, Canada's tally was the lowest in ODI history, but this record low has since been broken by Zimbabwe, who scored 35 against Sri Lanka in Harare in April 2004. This was the third shortest ODI of all time. The shortest completed ODI also involved Sri Lanka and Zimbabwe, in Colombo in December 2001, and lasted 120 balls.

Total team-fail

The South African scorecard in the first Test against England at Edgbaston in June 1924 made for strange reading, as not a single batsman made double figures. This is the only time in Test history that all 11 players in a team have failed to get into double figures.

South Africa were skittled for a meagre 30 runs in their first innings. 'Extras' was the highest scorer with 11, followed by opener and captain, Herbie Taylor, who managed seven. The innings included four ducks. Needless to say, England won the match by an innings.

Close, but no ton at lunch

No South African batsman has made a century before lunch on the first day of a Test match – though Barry Richards came agonisingly close. In the second Test against Australia in Durban in February 1970, Richards was on 94 in the over before lunch, with captain Ali Bacher facing. Bacher tried to nudge a single to give Richards the strike, but was bowled around his legs by Alan Connolly for nine, three balls before the break.

Only four batsmen have reached three figures by lunch on the first day of a Test match – Australia's Charles Macartney (112 by lunch against England in 1926); Pakistan's Majid Khan (108 by lunch against New Zealand in 1976); Australia's Don Bradman (105 by lunch against England in 1930); and Australia's Victor Trumper (103 by lunch against England in 1902).

If you can keep your head ...

South African opener Bernard Tancred set a record in the second Test match ever played by South Africa, which still stands today. He holds the record for the least number of runs scored by an opening Test batsman who carried his bat through a completed innings. In the second Test between South Africa and England in Cape Town in March 1889, Tancred scored just 26 runs in South Africa's first-innings score of 47 all out. He also became the first batsman in Test history to carry his bat through a completed Test innings.

The next highest scorer was the South African captain William Milton, who scored 7 as England won the match by an innings and 202 runs. Only four other South African batsmen have carried their bats in a Test innings: Billy Zulch (43 not out against England in Cape Town in March 1910); Trevor Goddard (56 not out against Australia in Cape Town in December 1957); Jackie McGlew (127 not out against New Zealand in Durban in December 1961); and Gary Kirsten (100 not out against Pakistan in Faisalabad in October 1997).

An eight-ton blitz

The fourth Test between South Africa and the West Indies at St John's in Antigua in 2005 set the record for the most centuries in a Test: eight in total. There were four in the South African first innings: AB de Villiers (114), Graeme Smith (126), Jacques Kallis (147) and Ashwell Prince (131). The West Indies got four in their first innings, including a triple century (317) by Chris Gayle. The other centurions were Ramnaresh Sarwan (127), Shivnarine Chanderpaul (127) and Dwayne Bravo (107).

No ducks for Kepler

Kepler Wessels holds the record for having played the most ODIs without ever going out for a duck. He played in 109 ODIs – 54 for Australia and 55 for South Africa. He managed to get off the mark every time, with a lowest score of 1 seven times. His top score was 107 and his ODI average a respectable 34.35.

The rarest of king pairs

Getting a king pair – a first-ball duck in both innings – in a Test match is a relatively rare event, but none comes rarer than South African wicketkeeper Tommy Ward's king pair in a Test match between South Africa and Australia at Old Trafford, Manchester, in May 1912. The match was part of a triangular tournament. In the first innings, Ward, batting at number 11, was out LBW to Jimmy Matthews for a duck to give Matthews a hat-trick. In the second innings, Ward, batting at number nine, was out caught and bowled by Matthews for a duck for the king pair. Amazingly, Ward's dismissal gave Matthews another hat-trick. Hence Matthews achieved the rare feat of two hat-tricks in a Test match, both on the same day, but, most astonishingly, Ward was his hat-trick victim on each occasion.

Other South Africans who got king pairs in Test matches are Bert Vogler in the first Test against Australia in Sydney in December 1910 (the first man to 'achieve' the feat in Test cricket); Colin 'Tich' Wesley against England in the third Test in Nottingham in July 1960; and Dave Richardson against Pakistan in the one-off Test in Johannesburg in January 1995.

Not easily stumped

South African wicketkeeper Dave Richardson holds the record for the highest number of Test catches by a wicketkeeper before his first Test stumping. Richardson took 119 Test catches before finally getting his first stumping in his 33rd Test match, against India in Cape Town in January 1997. He ended the drought by whipping off the bails to dismiss Venkatesh Prasad off Paul Adams's bowling and give South Africa a 282-run victory. Richardson would get just one more stumping, in his third last Test match, though he took 150 catches in his 42 Tests.

Richardson was a lot quicker to get his first stumping in an ODI, achieving that feat in his very first ODI with just his second international dismissal. He stumped Mohammad Azharuddin off Tim Shaw's bowling in South Africa's first ODI after readmission to the ICC against India at Eden Gardens on 10 November 1991. He took 148 catches and 17 stumpings in 122 ODIs.

A controversial declaration

The lowest first-innings score by a team which went on to win a Test match is no runs at all. This occurred in the controversial fifth Test between South Africa and England in Centurion in January 2000. South Africa scored 155 for 6 when play was halted after just 45 overs on the first day due to rain. No play was possible for the next three days. On the final day, South Africa were to resume batting in a match that would inevitably end in a dull draw. Then Hansie Cronje made what was initially thought to have been a brave, bold and innovative move to make a game of it, but which has subsequently been exposed as one of the more despicable motives in Test cricket.

Half an hour before the start of play on the final day, Cronje offered a run chase to England captain Nasser Hussain if England were prepared to forfeit their first innings and South Africa would forfeit their second innings. Cronje declared South Africa's first innings on 248 for 8, leaving England to score 249 in 76 overs. The scorers officially recorded England's first innings and South Africa's second innings as nought for no wicket declared, even though the players never took the field. England reached the winning target with five balls to spare for a famous victory. But the effusive praise for Cronje changed five months later, when it was revealed at the King Commission inquiry into match fixing that Cronje had received over R50,000 and a leather jacket from a bookmaker who had persuaded him to get a result in the match. Cronje maintained he had acted in the best interests of the match, and that the crowds needed to be entertained – even though South Africa's 14-match winning streak had come to an end. However, the match will only be remembered as the first Test match in which it was proved that match fixing had taken place.

A long wait between Tests

South African and Zimbabwean spin bowler John Traicos has the record for the longest gap between Test matches – a remarkable 22 years and 222 days. Born in the exotically named Zigazag in Egypt, Traicos grew up in South Africa and played for the South African Universities team which toured England in 1967. He settled in what was then Rhodesia, and, at a time when Rhodesians were picked for both the Springbok cricket and rugby teams, he made his debut for South Africa in the second Test against Australia in Durban in February 1970. He earned a further two caps in the third and fourth Tests in Johannesburg and Port Elizabeth. The St George's Test was the last Test match South Africa would play before international isolation. When Zimbabwe became a fully fledged Test-playing nation in 1992, Traicos was eligible for selection. At the relatively old age – for a cricketer, in any case – of 45, he played in Zimbabwe's inaugural Test against India in Harare in October 1992, taking 5 for 86 in 50 overs.

While John Traicos played on cricket's big stage, his daughter played on a stage that was actually a stage. Chloe Traicos moved to Australia in 1998 with her family from Zimbabwe, where she was born and raised, as soon as she had finished school, settling in Perth. She later moved to Sydney and made a name for herself as an actress, film director and screenwriter.

She won the New York Film Festival award for best director for her acclaimed documentary, 'A Stranger in My Homeland', which featured Zimbabwean refugees living in Australia, and was a protest against the situation in the country of her birth.

Unsuccessful spin

The worst figures by a South African bowler who failed to take a wicket in a Test match belong to spin bowler Nicky Boje. In the first Test between Sri Lanka and South Africa in Colombo in July 2006, Boje bowled 65 overs, including five maidens, conceded 221 runs and took no wickets. Despite the poor record, the highly regarded oracle of cricket, *Wisden*, reported that Boje had been the most effective of the bowlers, operating over the wicket for much of the innings and directing the ball into the rough. What didn't make matters any easier for Boje is that he was bowling to Kumar Sangakkara and Mahela Jayawardene as they were setting a world-record third-wicket stand of 624 runs. Need we add that Sri Lanka won the match by an innings and 53 runs?

Happily for Boje, his figures are not the worst for a Test bowler. That ignominy belongs to Pakistan's Khan Mohammad, who recorded 0 for 259 from 54 overs against the West Indies in Kingston in March 1958. Poor Mohammad had to watch the great Garry Sobers rack up 365 not out, which, at the time, was the world Test batting record.

Success reaps no reward

Two South African cricketers can feel slightly aggrieved about having been dropped from the Test side – after turning in career-best performances. Syd Burke took an extraordinary 11 wickets in his debut Test for South Africa, the third Test against New Zealand, in Cape Town in January 1962. Burke, a fast bowler from north-eastern Transvaal, was initially expensive in the New Zealand first innings, taking 2 for 110 in 16 overs, but took a further four wickets on the second day of the match to finish with 6 for 128 in 53.3 overs. In New Zealand's second innings, he took five wickets for 68 runs – a match haul of 11 for 196. But Burke's performance wasn't enough to prevent defeat for South Africa by 72 runs. It was a famous New Zealand victory – only their second in their Test history and their first abroad. Burke's heroics didn't endear him, however, to the selectors, who opted to recall Peter Heine after three years of absence from the international game to team up with his old partner, Neil Adcock, who had recovered from injury. There was no need for another fast bowler, and Burke carried the drinks in the fourth Test before being dropped altogether. He played one more Test match three years later, taking no wickets.

Pat Symcox was dropped after scoring 108 in the first Test against Pakistan at the Wanderers in February 1998, one of the few players in Test history to be dropped after scoring a century. He had joined debutant Mark Boucher at the wicket, with South Africa struggling on 166 for 8. They put on a world-record 195 for the ninth wicket, with Symcox scoring his century on the morning of the second day. He became only the third number ten in the world to score a Test ton, and the first in 96 years. But Symcox was selected as a spin bowler, not a batsman, and the selectors decided they needed a bit of pace for the second Test in Durban, and he was replaced by Fanie de Villiers. Symcox played three more Tests for South Africa before retiring.

Unique failure and success in one Test

South Africa's Dudley Nourse is the only Test batsman to have recovered from the embarrassment of a first-innings duck to score a double century in the second innings. In the second Test against Australia in Johannesburg in December 1935, Nourse was bowled for a duck as South Africa were skittled for 157. Chasing a first-innings deficit of 93 runs, Nourse made amends for his first-innings failure by racking up 231 runs in South Africa's innings of 491. The match ended in a draw.

A poor start

Three South Africans go down in history as having the most inauspicious of Test careers. Yet their remarkable names will live on – Clarence Wimble, Percy Twentyman-Jones and Plum Lewis. They all played in one Test match, got a pair (no runs in either innings) and took no wickets and no catches. Wimble's mediocrity was against England in Cape Town in March 1892, Twentyman-Jones's against Australia in Cape Town in November 1902 and Lewis's in Durban in December 1913. Although Twentyman-Jones and Lewis may not have made a mark in international cricket, they certainly made their names in other fields. Twentyman-Jones played football for South Africa and went on to become the Judge-President of the Cape Division of the Supreme Court. Lewis became a decorated soldier, serving in France in World War I, where he was awarded the Military Cross and Bar for bravery.

A lack of runs, catches and wickets in a Test career of just one match is not exclusively the stuff of a bygone age, however. Spare a thought for England's Gavin Hamilton, who managed the 'feat' against South Africa in Johannesburg in November 1999. Like Wimble, Twentyman-Jones and Lewis before him, Hamilton played in only one Test match and non-achieved with no runs (a duck in both innings, having faced a total of nine balls), no wickets (15 overs, 1 maiden, 0 for 63) and no catches (history doesn't record if he dropped any).

South African George Thornton's only Test match was slightly more memorable: he scored one run, took one wicket and took one catch against Australia in Johannesburg in October 1902.

No follow-on means no win

The only time a team chose not to enforce the follow-on in a Test match, and then managed to lose the match occurred in Durban during the third Test between South Africa and Australia in January 1950. In the first innings, South Africa scored 311 and then skittled Australia for 75, with Hugh Tayfield taking 7 for 23. South Africa's captain Dudley Nourse, despite having the option of enforcing the follow-on with a first-innings advantage of 236 runs, fatefully decided to bat again. He had had the whole day to think about the decision, as Sunday was a rest day. South Africa collapsed dismally to 99 all out, with eight batsmen falling for 14 runs to give Australia a target of 336 to win. Australia reached the winning target with just five wickets down, thanks largely to Neil Harvey's 151 in five and a half hours, which, at the time, was considered to be one of the greatest Test innings.

The *Wisden* report said: 'This innings of extraordinary patience and skill ... left a lasting impression upon all who witnessed it. The history of Test cricket provides few comparable feats.'

Nourse was widely criticised for not enforcing the follow-on, but received support for the decision from the Australian captain Lindsay Hassett, who said he would have made the same decision.

Madonna's greatest fan?

When Gary Kirsten retired from international cricket, he had played in 101 Test matches (with a batting average of 45.27) and 185 ODIs (with a batting average of 40.95). He was always destined to play for South Africa, but his career got a kick-start from American pop star Madonna.

Madonna had performed three shows of her Girlie Show Tour at the Melbourne Cricket Ground on 26, 27 and 29 November 1993. Five days later, at the same venue, South Africa played Victoria in a four-day warm-up match before the first Test against Australia, which was to start on Boxing Day. After enduring thousands of dancing pop fans for three days, the outfield was very uneven. Brian McMillan fell victim to the poor surface while fielding, and was injured to the extent that he couldn't finish bowling his 13th over. He would need a couple of weeks to recover, and Kirsten was flown out to cover for him.

Kirsten was brought into the South African side for his ODI debut against Australia in Sydney on 14 December, scoring four runs. He then made his Test debut, along with Fanie de Villiers, in the Boxing Day Test at the MCG, scoring 16 in the rain-plagued draw. He went on to enjoy one of the most illustrious of careers, and we have to wonder if he ever thanks Madonna and her fans for giving him the break.

The day-night game
that finished in the day

The first international cricket match under lights had an inauspicious start at Newlands in Cape Town on 10 December 1986, when the match was over before the lights could be switched on. The sun goes down very late in summer in the Cape, and the match between a South African XI and an Australian XI ended with the sun still shining. South Africa bowled out the Australians for 85 in 34 overs, with Garth le Roux taking 6 for 21. The South Africans then took just 15 overs to reach the winning target with eight wickets in hand.

The short of it

South Africa was involved in the shortest Test match in history – 109 overs and two balls long. The match was the rain-plagued fifth Test against Australia in Melbourne in 1932. The persistent rain meant only five hours and 53 minutes of play was possible from 12 to 15 February. In an era of uncovered wickets, the rain had turned the wicket into a monster. In their first innings, South Africa were bowled out for 36 in 23.2 overs. In reply, Australia managed 153 in 54.3 overs. South Africa's second innings lasted just 31.3 overs, as they were skittled for 45, and Australia won the match by an innings and 72 runs.

Jubilation and humiliation

South African fast bowler Geoff Griffin made his mark in Test history in two remarkable and widely differing events, both of which happened in the same Test match. The story starts with Griffin breaking his right arm as a schoolboy. The fracture wasn't set properly, and Griffin couldn't physically straighten the arm ever again. Griffin was a gifted fast bowler, but because of the angle of his right arm, umpires began to target him for chucking. He became the first player to be no-balled in a first-class match, when Natal took on Transvaal in Durban in the 1958/59 season. Despite the concern over his action, Griffin was selected for the South African side to tour England in 1960. His action passed scrutiny in four tour matches before a match against the MCC, during which both umpires called him for throwing. Griffin and his captain Jackie McGlew were confused because one of the umpires had previously passed 180 of Griffin's deliveries without objection.

Officials and umpires held a meeting, with the media putting pressure on the MCC to make a final decision on Griffin's action. In South Africa's next tour match, against Nottinghamshire, Griffin was no-balled again and he was sent to former England fast bowler Alf Glover for three days of coaching. Griffin got through his next tour match and the first Test in Birmingham before being hauled up yet again in a tour match against Hampshire.

But in the second Test at Lord's in June 1960, the controversy came to a head. He became the first bowler to be no-balled for throwing in a Test in England, and only the third in Test history. Griffin was no-balled 11 times in the match, but amid the 'throwing' controversy, he was at the centre of a sensational achievement, becoming the first person to get a hat-trick at Lord's. England had racked up a big score of 347 for 5 as day two was coming to a close, when South African captain Jackie McGlew brought Griffin on in the final half-hour of play.

Mike Smith was not out on 99 and on the last ball of one of Griffin's overs he edged the ball to wicketkeeper Johnny Waite. With the first ball of his following over, Griffin clean bowled Peter Walker for 52. The next batsman was the England fast bowler Freddie Trueman. Since Smith's wicket had fallen in Griffin's previous over, Trueman didn't realise that he was facing the hat-trick ball. He took a huge swipe at the delivery and was bowled. As the crowd cheered the first ever Test hat-trick at cricket's hallowed sanctuary, Lord's, McGlew had to inform Griffin of his achievement. He too had forgotten he was on a hat-trick.

McGlew wrote poignantly about Griffin's historic achievement, reached as he surely felt his Test career was to be no-balled into oblivion: 'Griffin took it very calmly, in much the same way as he had accepted the infinitely harder moments of this tour. If he ever had such ambitions as a Test match cricketer, he could surely not have dreamed of their fulfilment here at Lord's.'

Since the Test match finished on the afternoon of the fourth day, with England winning by an innings and 73 runs, both teams agreed to play an exhibition match. This proved to be the end of Griffin's tour and ultimately his Test career. Umpire Syd Buller called him four times for throwing. In order for Griffin to end his over, he decided to bowl underarm. However, he was no-balled again, this time by umpire Frank Lee. Griffin had forgotten to tell the batsman he was changing to underarm.

Griffin played two seasons of provincial cricket for Rhodesia, but umpires continued to no-ball him, prompting him to retire. He died of a heart attack in Durban in 2006, aged 67.

The beer at the end of the day

During South Africa's third tour match of the 1963/64 tour of Australia against a Combined Western Australia XI in November 1963, Eddie Barlow was determined to make his mark. He had failed in the first innings, scoring just three runs. When he went out to open South Africa's second innings at 1.40pm, he told his teammates: 'See you at six o'clock, chaps – and have a cold beer ready.'

True to his word, Barlow was not out and the next day he reached 209 before Richie Benaud had him caught and bowled. Barlow's knock broke the record of 204 for a South African batsman against Australia, set by Aubrey Faulkner in 1910. Barlow had also broken his own first-class record of 118. When congratulated on breaking the record for a South African batsman in Australia, Barlow took off his glasses, wiped his brow and asked, 'What record?'

Another remarkable statistic from this match is Graeme Pollock's second-innings knock of 127, which he scored between lunch and tea in 108 minutes and which included 22 fours.

Leaping from leagues to Tests

Making the jump from playing league cricket to Test cricket is certainly a meteoric rise in any cricketer's fortunes. This is what happened to an English cricketer, Ken Palmer, a Somerset medium-pacer, who was playing for Old Marists in the somewhat lowly, yet competitive, club league in Johannesburg in February 1965, when he got a surprising call-up to the England team. Mike Smith's team had suffered some injury problems after a long tour, with Bob Barber having returned home, John Price having strained stomach muscles and Tom Cartwright battling with a damaged knee. Being the fifth and final Test of the series in Port Elizabeth, there was no time to fly out a replacement. Since Palmer was coaching and playing in South Africa, he was told to make his way to St George's Park to make his Test debut. It was Palmer's only Test match as a player; in it he took 1 for 113 and the match ended in a draw.

One of England's top bowlers, the fiery and bombastic Fred Trueman, had inexplicably been left out of the England team, and at the time of the fifth Test, he was touring the West Indies with an International Cavaliers side, sponsored by the cigarette company Rothmans. He had been replaced in the England team by Ian Thompson. When Trueman heard that Palmer had been called up to the England team as the late bowling replacement, he raged: 'While Thompson and Palmer are opening the bowling for England, I'm here playing for cigarette coupons!'

Palmer went on to have an illustrious 30-year career as a county cricket umpire, standing in 22 Test matches and 23 ODIs.

We fast-forward to the fifth and final Test between England and

Australia in Manchester in August 1981. The Australians, like the Englishmen in South Africa in 1965, were also at the end of a long tour and battling with injury problems. Mike Whitney, a 22-year-old from New South Wales, was playing club cricket for the fishing village of Fleetwood in the Northern Lancashire League. He had a good trial match for Gloucestershire, and received a call-up to make his Test debut for Australia in the fifth Test against England at Old Trafford. From Lancashire league to a Test debut – not unlike the meteoric rise of Ken Palmer. And umpiring in Whitney's debut Test – who else but Ken Palmer?

Out without facing a legal ball

The scorecard for the first T20 International between the West Indies and South Africa, played on 19 May 2010 at the Sir Vivian Richards Stadium, North Sound, Antigua, has the unusual entry of: Narsingh Deonarine st De Villiers, b Botha 0 (1 minute, 0 balls). The question is: how can he have faced '0 balls', if he was in fact stumped by AB de Villiers off Johan Botha's bowling? The answer is that he was stumped off the first ball he faced, and that ball was called a wide. According to Cricinfo, this could be only the third time a batsman has been stumped in an international cricket match without facing a legal ball.

Many maidens bowled over

In the third Test against England in Durban in January 1957, South African spin bowler Hugh Tayfield bowled 16 consecutive eight-ball overs, without conceding a run. In fact, he bowled 137 consecutive balls without a run being scored off him – a world record for first-class cricket. His first-innings analysis was an incredible 24 overs, 17 maidens, 21 runs, one wicket. The match ended in a draw.

Top-scoring tail-ender

South African spin bowler Bert Vogler's knock of 62 not out in the fifth Test against England in Cape Town in March/April 1906 goes down in the record books. It was the first time in a Test match that a number 11 batsman had got the top score in his team's innings. The feat has now been achieved seven times in Tests, with Vogler's knock being the highest of the seven tail-enders on that list.

Kapil vs Kirsten

Peter Kirsten could be an obstinate player, but it resulted in his being fined half his match fee in an acrimonious second one-day international between South Africa and India in Port Elizabeth on 9 December 1992. Earlier in the Indian tour, the great Indian all-rounder Kapil Dev had warned Kirsten against backing up too far. Matters came to a head at St George's Park, with South Africa chasing a meagre 148 for victory. Looking for a quick wicket, and without the customary warning, Kapil stopped in mid-delivery while Kirsten was advancing down the pitch, and quickly knocked off the bails at his end. The umpire had no choice but to give Kirsten out, but initially he refused to walk, protesting that he believed it to be unsportsmanlike behaviour.

Although this type of dismissal is within the laws of the game, it's considered unsporting to run a player out in such a way without a prior warning. Kirsten eventually walked off, but the incident had soured the match, and the acrimony bubbled over as the South African captain Kepler Wessels collided with Kapil while completing a run. Kapil complained that Wessels had deliberately hit him on the shins with his bat. Wessels claimed it was an accident, but the Indian players saw it as deliberate retribution for having run Kirsten out. The match referee Clive Lloyd was called on to adjudicate. He hadn't seen the incident, and the TV footage shed no further light on the matter, as the cameras were following the ball at the time. South Africa won the match by six wickets.

Anyone for tennis?

Two South African cricketers, Kepler Wessels and AB de Villiers, could well have ended up as tennis professionals or Test rugby players, such was their prodigious talent for sport. De Villiers was once ranked second in the country as a 12-year-old tennis player. He lost interest in the game in Standard 7, but credits his mother, who was his coach, with giving him the mental stamina to cope in top-flight cricket. The two travelled around the country as AB played in local tournaments. At the age of 13, he was offered an opportunity to attend the legendary Nick Bollettieri's Tennis Academy in Florida, but his parents thought he was too young to go. De Villiers could have turned his attention to rugby and played for the Blue Bulls junior team when he was 18. He considered an offer to sign for them, but had already decided on a career in cricket.

As a rugby player, the young Kepler Wessels played fullback for the Free State primary schools team, playing in curtain-raisers for the Currie Cup clashes at the Free State Stadium in Bloemfontein where he was attending school at Grey College. In one match against Northern Transvaal Schoolboys, Wessels's opposite number broke through the Free State defence, but instead of heading for the line to score a try, pulled up short and slotted a drop kick. The boy was Naas Botha.

But Wessels soon gave up rugby for tennis. Like AB de Villiers, Wessels competed on a nationwide circuit of tournaments for teenagers, and was trained by a well-known coach at the time, Lou Sylvester. By 1973, Wessels was ranked the number-one under-16 player in South Africa. One of his big rivals was Johan Kriek, with honours roughly even in all the matches they played. Kriek went on to win two Grand Slam titles – both at the Australian Open.

Wessels was offered a scholarship by the University of Houston in December 1973. He was encouraged by the great South African Davis Cup player Eric Sturgess who worked with Wessels as part of an elite national squad. But the fiercely competitive Wessels had started to compete in senior competitions aged just 16 and found it frustrating when he started to lose more regularly. He finally snapped during the Griqualand West Open against Cyril Rudman, stormed off the court at the end of the match and slashed the strings of his racket with a pair of scissors. Cricket became his sport of choice.

Wessels and AB de Villiers are not the only cricketers who had to make a choice between sports. Eddie Barlow was also a decent rugby player in his younger days before deciding to chuck it in for the willow.

He played first-team rugby at Pretoria Boys' High and when he left school to study at Wits University he played both sports for a while, before deciding to retire from cricket and give some more time to his studies. His retirement lasted all of a week, when he was asked to fill in for a residence team, and was then picked for the first XI.

Sport took priority from then on, and Barlow found himself in the Wits under-19 team and was one of eight picked to play for the Transvaal under-19 side in his first year. The next year, he was picked for the Transvaal under-20 team, where he played alongside the late Frederik van Zyl Slabbert, the great politician and voice of reason whom Barlow described as being his 'political mentor'.

In 1960, Barlow was chosen for both the Transvaal rugby and cricket senior teams, although he won his provincial cap for rugby first and was picked to play against the touring All Blacks at the old Ellis Park stadium. In 1960, the stadium was a lot more open and basic, but could seat 100,000, and this day there was close on that number, according to Barlow.

Playing at centre, Barlow's shirt was still brilliantly white as the All Blacks were thumping Transvaal and the ball had barely got near the backline.

In the second half, Terry Lineen, the All Blacks flyhalf, put in a chip from an All Blacks scrum. Barlow jumped and caught the ball and as he began to congratulate himself, was hit in mid-air and carried from the Transvaal 25-yard line to just short of the tryline and then thumped to the ground.

'Feeling as if I should somehow defend my honour, I turned around to find the substantial figure of Colin "Pinetree" Meads lying beside me. Without thinking, I pulled back my right arm ready to strike.'

'"Don't!" said the legendary All Black.'

'So I didn't. I was the laughing stock of the entire Transvaal team after the game and it must have looked odd to see this little squirt of a student attempting to rearrange the features of so great a rugby man.'

Despite having 12 Springboks in their starting XV that day, Transvaal were beaten 19-13.

In April 1962, Barlow was struggling to keep up with the demands of playing provincial rugby and cricket, and upon advice from friends decided to concentrate on cricket ... after one more season.

The British and Irish Lions were in town that year and Barlow fancied a crack at playing them. He was picked for the Northern Universities team to play the Lions at the PAM Brink stadium in Springs. Danie Craven, President of the South African Rugby

Board, paid the team a visit in their dressing room shortly before the match and gave them a motivational talk that was pure Craven: 'Listen, if you don't do better than the last Northern Universities team, then you won't play a touring side again.' He then punched every player on the shoulder. 'And if you don't play well, then you are going to get more of this.'

The students played well, motivated by Craven, and earned a 6-6 draw. They could have won had they not missed three penalties, but not before Barlow had experienced his own exceptionally embarrassing moment. Facing up to Alan Jones, the Welsh centre, Barlow moved up to tackle him, but Jones sidestepped beautifully and Barlow fell flat on his face 'in front of 30,000 people'.

Barlow remembered his centre partner running past, and in a quote that has been used several times down the years, was told: 'You've got to watch these okes, Eddie, because they are ambidextrous in both feet.'

Barlow said some of the Lions told him he was the best centre they had played against, but his mind was made up, and he retired from rugby in September 1962.

Barry Richards teaches
Morné du Plessis

Barlow did come into contact with another rugby player in his playing career, though, when he moved down to Western Province. He was asked to play for the Stellenbosch University Cricket Club, and found they had a certain tall player called Morné du Plessis. Also in that side were Mike Procter and André Bruyns.

Indeed, the rugby connection went to the top of Western Province cricket, as Barlow found that the only member of the Province Board that he knew was Billy Louw, against whom he had played at Loftus Versfeld in a school game between Pretoria Boys' High and Rondebosch.

As well as Garth le Roux, Barlow remembered a talented young fast bowler who had been with the team for a short while before deciding to channel his efforts into rugby.

Morné du Plessis toured with Barlow and Province to Rhodesia where, said Barlow, he 'bowled very tidily and took quite a few wickets, and then came out with a remark that cheered those of us old dogs fielding in the slips – "I like bowling in this side because when the ball is caught in our slips it looks like it has hit a wall of putty. Everything sticks."'

Du Plessis's first-class career was spread over two seasons, 1971/72 and 73/74, and in his five matches he scored 24 runs with a high score of 16 and an average of 4.80. He took 16 wickets at an average of 25.62 and his best figures were 4 for 71. That's 801 balls bowled and 410 runs scored off them. It wasn't to last.

'When you go to Stellenbosch to play cricket, it is like going to India to play rugby. You realise very quickly that rugby is the game in Stellenbosch, just as cricket is in India,' said Du Plessis, whose dad had captained the Springboks.

'I decided I must give rugby a go. After my under-20 year, I got into the first team as a lock forward. Doc [Danie Craven] was away on one of his numerous rugby sojourns. When he returned and the team was read to him, he decided that I couldn't play lock because I was not big enough. He saw me as an eighth man.'

Du Plessis was picked for the Springboks in 1971, but admitted that the great Barry Richards also played a role in making his mind up about which sport to choose. He bowled to Richards when Natal visited Newlands and was punished.

'He was batting on the first day of a three-day Castle Cup match and in the final over before lunch, he hit me for two sixes into the railway stand. The over before lunch is usually when you block the bowler out. I realised then that rugby was probably a better way of defending myself.'

Gibbs flies the flag

Herschelle Gibbs established a world record in an ODI between South Africa and Pakistan in Sharjah on 28 March 2000. In a dismal performance by the South African batsmen, Gibbs scored 59 off 79 balls as his side was dismissed for 101. Five South Africans made ducks. The South African total became the lowest in the history of ODI cricket to include a half-century. Pakistan won the match easily by 67 runs.

No ducks

South Africa's total of 83 all out in the second ODI against England at Trent Bridge, Nottingham, on 26 August 2008 was unusual in that no one scored a duck. In fact, it was the second-lowest team total of a match in which no player was out without scoring. André Nel top-scored with 13 (and surely reminded the top order about this a few times), and Makhaya Ntini was not out for 0. England took an hour to knock off the winning runs without losing a wicket.

The lowest all-out total in one-day internationals that didn't involve anyone getting a duck is 54, scored by India against Sri Lanka in the final of the Coca-Cola Champions on 29 October 2000 in Sharjah. The lowest all-out total without a duck in a Test is 75, by Australia against South Africa in Durban in January 1950, when Hugh Tayfield took 7 for 23. That total included a 1 and five 2s; only three batsmen got double figures.

A low score beats a high score

When South Africa and New Zealand played to a draw in the second Test match in Christchurch in March 1999, South Africa's lowest individual scorer made more runs than New Zealand's highest individual scorer. In South Africa's first (and only) innings, Gary Kirsten scored 65 – the lowest score of the innings after 211 by Herschelle Gibbs and 148 by Jacques Kallis, as South Africa racked up 442 for 1 declared. By comparison, the highest score by a New Zealander in that match was made by Matthew Horne, with 56 in his side's second innings.

Centurions in Centurion

The first Test between South Africa and New Zealand at SuperSport Park – in the appropriately named town of Centurion – in April 2006 saw three players reach the milestone of 100 Test caps – Jacques Kallis and Shaun Pollock for South Africa and captain Stephen Fleming for New Zealand. Kallis scored 100 runs in the match (38 and 62), whereas Fleming had a poor game, getting a fifth-ball duck to the eventual man of the match, Makhaya Ntini. For the record, Pollock scored 24 and 10, and took two wickets. South Africa won the match by 128 runs.

The tireless, timeless Tim Heaney

The cricketing exploits of Old Parktonians and Transvaal bowler Tim Heaney are so remarkable that he was often described as the best left-arm bowler never to have played for South Africa.

In one match (the date of which is not clear, though it was probably played in the late 1940s), Heaney was playing for Old Parks against the Johannesburg railways team, JSAR, at Milner

Park. Old Parks had scored a modest 103, and JSAR were looking comfortable at 45 for 2 in reply.

According to a newspaper report of the match, odds of 100-1 on an Old Parks victory had been laid, and Heaney, sheltering in the outfield under a battered panama hat, loved a gamble.

Old Parks captain Lal Sadler threw Heaney the ball. He removed the big hat and proceeded to bowl three match-winning overs. So devastating was Heaney's bowling that he took the last eight JSAR wickets without conceding a single run. So amazing was his effort that four times he was on a hat-trick. In the first over, he took two wickets in succession. In the second over, he took four wickets in pairs and in the third over, he took wickets with another two successive deliveries.

The report says Heaney was showered with congratulations as he walked off the field, but '[i]nstead of a beaming broad smile he wore a disappointed look that he did not get at the man laying the 100-to-one odds'.

Heaney was described as a casual left-arm bowler who wore a pair of thick spectacles and shuffled rather than ran his eight paces to the wicket. He had a late whipping action through the last 45 centimetres of his bowling arc, which gave his deliveries deceptive pace. He was also deadly accurate and a master of spin.

In another undated club match for Old Parks against Old Edwardians, he took four wickets in four balls, and took a further two wickets in four balls – six wickets in eight deliveries. Every one of his victims was clean bowled and he finished with a match analysis of 8 for 13.

Heaney started playing for Transvaal as a 20-year-old before

World War II and enjoyed a provincial career of 17 years. One of his biggest games for his province was when Transvaal came close to beating Lindsay Hassett's Australians at Ellis Park in December 1949.

Australia batted first on a rain-damaged pitch, and Transvaal spin bowler Athol Rowan took a remarkable 9 for 19 as the tourists were reduced to 84 all out. Heaney took the ninth wicket, depriving Rowan of the magical ten wickets in an innings.

Transvaal had a relatively healthy 41-run lead when Australia batted again. Rowan once again proved to be the Aussies' undoing, taking 6 for 49. Heaney mopped up with 4 for 46, and Transvaal were in sight of a famous victory, requiring 69 to win. But on that tricky wicket, Transvaal capitulated and were bowled for just 53 to lose by 15 runs, despite the incredible performance of Rowan – 15 wickets for 68 runs.

Heaney was probably close to selection for the South African Test team that season, but the selectors opted for Tufty Mann, and he never played international cricket. He was often criticised by his teammates for an apparent lack of interest in the game for which he had obvious talents. He retired from provincial cricket in 1952 at the age of 38.

However, his club cricket career continued. Aged 40, he drove to and from Witbank every weekend to play club cricket for Old Parktonians. In one match played in 1954 against Old Johannians he took 8 for 23, bewildering the batsmen with his pace and accuracy.

He was still grabbing the headlines 20 years later, aged 60, when he played for the Wilf Isaacs XI against the Holland Still Going Strong team, and took four wickets for 20 runs in 14 overs.

A newspaper article about this remarkable performance, headlined 'Heaney still has that magic touch', doesn't give the venue, but quotes former Springbok wicketkeeper Denis Lindsay, who kept wicket that day, as saying: 'I was simply amazed. Tim was so accurate he could have spun the ball on a five-cent piece.'

When in his 60s, Heaney was called out of retirement and out of the pub at Old Parktonians to play a match against Old Eds. At the wicket were two Transvaal players, Albie During and a young, cocky Kevin McKenzie. McKenzie wasn't aware of Heaney's past exploits, and as the veteran shuffled up to bowl, McKenzie charged down the wicket to slog him over extra cover. Heaney drew up short and glared at McKenzie. 'If you charge at me, young man, I will hit you between the eyes,' warned Heaney.

'Just bowl, old man!' retorted McKenzie. As Heaney shuffled up once again, McKenzie took two big strides down the pitch. Heaney tried to pole-axe him as McKenzie tried to hit him out of the park. The delivery flummoxed McKenzie and he popped the ball up to a fielder who was cowering, expecting McKenzie to bludgeon the ball, and failed to make the catch. McKenzie remained bamboozled as Heaney tied him up for a couple more overs before finally dismissing him. The young turk, who would later become famous for hooking West Indian fast bowlers without a protective helmet, walked back to the dressing room suitably chastised. The pub was in festive uproar, and that's where the old man retreated at the end of the Old Eds innings.

At the fall of Old Parks' ninth wicket and with a thunderstorm imminent, a well-oiled Heaney set off for the wicket, knowing the longer he took, the more likely rain would stop play and prevent an Old Eds' victory. His delaying tactics were extreme. He took a circuitous route via the tennis courts before eventually arriving at the stumps. After surveying the light, and having enquired of umpire Hayward Kidson whether an appeal had been made, Heaney decided to take strike, taking guard a metre outside leg stump. In slow movements, he inched slowly across to his centre guard position. He survived the remaining two balls of the over.

Albie During bowled five balls of the next over to Doug Neilson, and, on the sixth ball, Neilson attempted a single to farm the bowling. Realising the run was impossible, he sent Heaney back. Turning as fast as a 60-year-old man who has a few beers on board can, Heaney saw that he was in trouble and fell in order to make his ground, stretching his bat into the safety zone. During took off the bails and appealed, but Heaney was given not out. Lying outstretched on the pitch and keeping an eye on the approaching storm, Heaney decided he was most uncomfortable. He took his hand off the bat, and cradled his head in his hand, critically breaking the contact with his bat. Apologetically, During, who was wise to the rules, now removed a stump and politely enquired of Kidson, 'And how is that?' This time, Heaney was out. He dusted himself down, put an arm around the shoulder of the young During and remarked, 'That has never happened to me before, lad. Let's have a beer.'

In an article in the *Rand Daily Mail* of 5 November 1968, headlined 'Tim, tired, but still very much alive', Heaney described his bowling as 'something like riding a bicycle – you never really forget'.

Bacher's big match

The heroics of Athol Rowan weren't enough to give Transvaal a famous victory over Australia at Ellis Park in December 1949, and it would take a further 17 years for a provincial team to beat an Australian touring team. Given that Transvaal had come so close at Ellis Park against Hassett's men, it seems appropriate that Transvaal eventually got that significant victory in November 1966 against Bobby Simpson's tourists.

The match was one of Transvaal captain Ali Bacher's personal triumphs. He took four catches, including one off a full-blooded drive from Bob Cowper while fielding at silly mid-on, and scored 45 followed by a rare second-innings double ton of 235. He and Tiger Lance (107) scored 237 for the fourth wicket as Transvaal won the match by 76 runs. The Australians fought hard for a draw, with the last pair needing to hold out for half an hour to the close of play. The victory came with eight minutes left on the clock when Tony Tillim bowled Neil Hawke for the memorable victory.

The frog in the blender

No South African cricketer has had his bowling action debated more often than Paul Adams. Descriptions have varied from 'like a frog in a blender' to 'like someone trying to take the hubcaps off a speeding car'.

His action was quite extraordinary, with his body bent at almost

90 degrees, his head dipping down and his face looking up at the moment of delivery. He appeared not to be looking at the batsman as his arm looped from behind his body and over his left ear as he released the ball. His action was so unorthodox that he easily flummoxed batsmen facing him for the first time. He could flight the ball superbly, and had good variation of pace.

He learnt his cricket in the working-class suburb of Grassy Park in Cape Town, and his talents were immediately identified. He went to the Western Cape Cricket Academy run by Eddie Barlow, before making his provincial debut for Western Province against Northern Transvaal in November 1995, taking 8 for 190, including six wickets in the second innings. Two days later, he was playing for South African A against the touring England team in Kimberley where he took 4 for 65 and 5 for 116.

The national selectors were cautious in drafting Adams into the Test side, waiting until the fourth Test before naming him in the starting XI. He had played just five first-class matches for Western Province.

At 18, Adams became the youngest person to play Test cricket for South Africa when he was drafted into the side for the Boxing Day Test in Port Elizabeth in December 1995. He took 4 for 126 in the drawn Test.

He retired in October 2008, finishing with 134 wickets in 45 Tests – a Test average of 32.87. In all his first-class cricket he took 412 wickets at an average of 32.66. His best return in Tests was 7 for 128 against Pakistan in Lahore in October 2003.

A wondrous welcome

A touring team's arrival in a host country is often a low-key event, with possibly a few die-hard fans gathering at the airport to catch a glimpse of the bleary-eyed players pushing overloaded trolleys through the arrivals terminal before being whisked by a luxury bus to the team hotel.

However, the International Cricket Council's dramatic decision on 23 October 1991 to readmit South Africa, at the urging of India's cricket authorities, and a sudden invitation to tour India within a week, generated so much excitement in the cricket world that a quiet arrival in Calcutta was always unlikely.

Pakistan had cancelled a scheduled tour of India, and South Africa was asked to embark on a short replacement tour. The newly formed United Cricket Board had just four days to prepare for a three-match tour, and a hastily assembled squad under the captaincy of Clive Rice arrived in Calcutta on 8 November 1991.

The players were met on the tarmac at Dumdum Airport by Indian cricket officials, daubed with a tilaka on the forehead and ushered onto their bus, which, in normal circumstances, would have taken 20 minutes to get them to the Oberoi Hotel.

Unprecedented hysteria greeted the unprepared South Africans. The journey to the hotel took almost three hours. Tens of thousands of people lined the route, welcoming the South Africans. The bus was halted three times and Rice, along with administrators, Krish Mackerdhuj and Geoff Dakin, addressed the crowd from a small platform. At the hotel, policemen standing shoulder to shoulder created a path for the players to scramble from the bus to the sanctuary of the hotel, keeping the crowds at bay.

After a visit to Mother Teresa on the Saturday, the South Africans walked out onto the field at Eden Gardens the following day to be greeted by more than a hundred thousand spectators. Nerves were jangling for the South African openers Andrew Hudson and Jimmy Cook, and Hudson faced just two balls before being caught behind off Kapil Dev for a duck. India won the match by three wickets with more than six overs to spare.

The nick seen around the cricketing world

If that return to international cricket was dramatic, the start of South Africa's first ever World Cup match was even more extraordinary – beginning with the very first ball. The match was against Australia at the Sydney Cricket Ground on 26 February 1992.

Australia's captain Allan Border won the toss and elected to bat first. Allan Donald bowled South Africa's first ball to Geoff Marsh, which he nicked. Wicketkeeper Dave Richardson took the comfortable catch, moving towards first slip, so obvious was the deviation from the bat.

The South Africans screamed their appeal, while the capacity 45-thousand crowd at the SCG roared in disbelief. Marsh stood his ground, and umpire Brian Aldridge stood rigid – not out.

To South Africa's credit, they put the disappointment behind them, but the Australians never settled and they eventually scored 179 for 9 in 49 overs, a target South Africa reached with two overs to spare and for the loss of just one wicket – a convincing nine-wicket victory.

Later, when asked by Hansie Cronje (who made his debut that day) about his not-out decision, Aldridge admitted he never saw the nick because Donald was too fast for him. He was looking down for a no-ball, and when he looked up the ball was already in Richardson's gloves. The noise of the crowd had blocked out the sound of the nick.

There were further extraordinary moments in that World Cup, including Jonty Rhodes's diving run-out of Inzamam-ul-Haq, discussed earlier in the book ('A fielder flies into history'), and a dramatic semi-final ...

22 runs off one ball

South Africa qualified for the semi-finals of the 1992 World Cup after winning five and losing three log games, to finish third, setting up a match against England at the SCG.

The start of the match was delayed by half an hour because of rain, and when the innings ended (after a slow over rate) on 45 overs with England posting 252 for 6, the rain came down again.

The South African innings started on schedule and the batsmen picked off the runs slowly, before needing a chase of 46 from the final five overs, with six wickets down. The seventh wicket pair of Dave Richardson and Brian McMillan scored 14 off two overs before the rain started falling again. Chris Lewis battled to bowl the 43rd over with a wet ball, and the South Africans took ten runs off five balls, before the umpires ordered the players from the field.

South Africa now needed 22 runs from 13 balls. The game could go either way, but, bizarrely, TV schedulers determined the fate of the match, not the players, umpires or weather conditions. Because the matches were being played in accordance with a tight and inflexible TV schedule, the match had to end at a certain time.

The statisticians worked out that the delays had meant the South African target was reduced to 21, and there was time for just one more ball to complete Lewis's over. The giant scoreboard, which had read 'South Africa to win need 22 runs off 13 balls', now changed to read – incorrectly – '22 runs off 1 ball'.

The crowd booed their disgust that this great contest had been taken out of the hands of the cricketers. McMillan dropped a dead bat on Lewis's final delivery and South Africa had been knocked out of their first ever World Cup – the start of many more highly unsatisfactory ends to a South African campaign at a Cricket World Cup.

The debutant's golden duck

And then there's South Africa's first Test match on home soil in 22 years. Superstitious cricket fans might have noticed that the game started on Friday 13 November 1992, at Kingsmead in Durban.

The opponents were Mohammad Azharuddin's Indians embarking on what was known as the Friendship Tour – in keeping with a promise made by the United Cricket Board when India formally proposed South Africa's readmission to the ICC.

The pitch would provide a lively reception to the team batting first, and captain Kepler Wessels looked on in dismay when he saw he had lost the toss. Andrew Hudson came out to bat with the veteran Jimmy Cook, who, at the age of 39, was finally making his official Test debut.

Within seconds, Cook became the first Test debutant to be given out on the first ball of a Test match. He pushed forward to a ball from Kapil Dev to Sachin Tendulkar at third slip and was out without scoring. There was some doubt as to whether the ball had in fact carried, but the umpire raised his finger.

Kepler Wessels steadied the innings with a patient 118, and the match eventually ended in a draw.

Two other South Africans were out on the first ball of a Test, though not in their debut Tests: Eddie Barlow in the third Test at Kingsmead in January 1967, and Gary Kirsten against the West Indies at Newlands in Cape Town in January 1999.

South Africa was also involved in Test history's second debutant's golden duck. The West Indies' Leon Garrick, called up 24 hours before the start of the fifth Test at Sabina Park, Kingston, Jamaica, in 2001 was out first ball of his debut Test, caught by Shaun Pollock off Allan Donald's bowling.

South Africa's first Test on home soil after readmission featured a number of other firsts: Omar Henry was the oldest South African Test debutant, four months short of his 41st birthday;

Kepler Wessels scored 118 to become the first person to score Test centuries for two different countries (he scored 162 on debut for Australia); umpire Cyril Mitchley became the first umpire to give a batsman out in a Test match after assistance from the third umpire, Karl Liebenberg; and Sachin Tendulkar (run out for 11) was the TV umpire's first Test victim.

Walk!

What are the chances of a Test batsman, after being given out by an umpire, being recalled by the opposing team's captain? About as likely as a batsman 'walking' without an umpire signalling that he was out, caught after the faintest of nicks.

But there was a time when 'walking' was expected, and being recalled was … well, not that uncommon.

Both issues became controversial during the third and fourth Tests between South Africa and England in January 1965.

On the first day of the third Test on New Year's Day, Eddie Barlow, on 41, stretched forward to smother a ball from spinner Fred Titmus. The ball looped into the air and Peter Parfitt took the catch at short leg. Barlow stayed rooted in his crease as the England players shouted an appeal, which was turned down by umpire John Warner.

The England players were furious, insisting that Barlow had snicked the ball onto his boot, causing it to fly into the air and into Parfitt's eager hands for a legitimate bat-boot catch. Barlow and

Titmus exchanged angry words as the England players made a public show of their fury. The incident was all over the newspapers, both in South Africa and England as the debate about 'walking' raged on.

This was also the era when fielding sides acknowledged a batsman's century. But when Barlow reached his ton (eventually out for 138), the petulant England players stood with their hands on their hips or turned their backs. They later apologised for their actions.

Then in England's first innings on the third day, Ken Barrington, on 44, played a bump ball to Trevor Goddard and started walking grim-faced to the pavilion. He then abruptly turned back to his crease with a grin on his face. The players and spectators saw the funny side, but things got serious three runs later.

Barrington flashed at a lifting ball from Peter Pollock, and Denis Lindsay took the catch as the South Africans went up in appeal. Barrington took a step back and waited for umpire Warner's decision. Warner, as in Barlow's case, was unmoved. Barrington later said he knew he was out, and, after standing at the crease for a few more seconds, started walking off. He said it was a matter of principle and sportsmanship.

He got a mixed reaction from sports writers – some called it an act of chivalry, others labelled it an ostentatious display that insulted the umpire. Barrington later apologised to Warner for taking so long to walk. His dismissal was given as 'caught Lindsay, bowled Pollock'. The match ended in a draw.

That was the end of the 'to walk or not to walk' saga, but there was a new controversy in the fourth Test at the Wanderers a fortnight later. Batting in his side's first innings, the England captain Mike Smith let a ball from Joe Partridge go through to wicketkeeper John Waite, who threw the ball to Peter van der Merwe at leg slip while Smith left his crease to prod at the wicket. Van der Merwe saw that Smith was out of his crease and threw down the stumps. The square-leg umpire Hayward Kidson raised his finger. Smith stared at the umpire for several seconds and then started the long walk to the dressing room.

South Africa's captain Trevor Goddard ran over to talk urgently to Van der Merwe. He then turned to Kidson and said there was too much doubt in his mind over whether or not the run-out was fair, and asked if Smith could be recalled. Kidson agreed and hollered at Smith, who had reached the boundary, to return.

Smith resumed his innings, after a smile and a nod of thanks to Goddard, but Van der Merwe was seen muttering to Waite, clearly unhappy with the end result. Waite later said he considered the ball to be 'dead', but Van der Merwe remained convinced that, because Waite had taken the ball and flicked it to him in one move, the ball was still alive and the run-out was legitimate. Smith went on to score 42 in the drawn Test.

Time to retire

Transvaal batsman Henry Fotheringham was given out 'retired out' after deciding for himself that a catch had been fairly taken, although the umpire disagreed.

The incident happened in a Currie Cup match against Rhodesia at the Wanderers in January 1979. Fotheringham had ten runs to his name when he edged a ball into the slips. Umpire Syd Moore ruled that the catch was not legitimate and turned down the Rhodesian appeal. Fotheringham then asked the fielder if the catch was fair. The fielder said it was, and Fotheringham tucked his bat under his arm and walked off.

During the lunch break, umpire Moore went to the scorers' box and told them that the official entry should be 'Fotheringham, retired out, 10' − one of the rare occasions that a batsman has given himself out.

The sharp-tongued, big-hitting Tiger

A player with a sharp tongue to match his aggressive style of play was Tiger Lance. He set a South African record for the most sixes in an innings, when he bludgeoned ten of them in a knock of 122 for Transvaal against Eastern Province in Johannesburg in his side's second innings in November 1966.

His most famous six was when he thumped Ian Chappell into the grandstand to give South Africa a seven-wicket win in the fifth and final Test against Australia at St George's Park in February 1967 to wrap up a 3-1 series victory for South Africa. The ball that Lance hit into the stands was returned to Eastern Province cricket officials years later by the spectator who had caught it. The ball was mounted and displayed in a glass case at St George's Park.

Lance's comments on and off the field are a mixture of fact and fiction. Playing for Wanderers in a league fixture against Old Edwardians, he was heard to remark to a teammate who had just been dismissed for a golden duck: 'Sorry I missed your innings. I blinked just then.'

Lance had a job with South African Breweries and was introducing a friend to a new beer on the market. The friend stared critically at his beer and said: 'Bit cloudy, isn't it?'

'What did you expect?' replied Lance. 'A storm?'

In his debut Test match against New Zealand at the Wanderers in February 1962, Lance was taking considerable punishment trying to dismiss John Reid, while the Kiwi captain was on his way to a second-innings knock of 142. In desperation, he turned to his skipper Jackie McGlew for advice. 'Keep it up to the bat and pray to God that he makes a mistake,' said McGlew.

'I can't,' moaned Lance. 'I think that's Him batting!'

Lance was involved in a dramatic last-wicket partnership with Athol McKinnon for Transvaal against Western Province at the Wanderers in December 1965. In the Transvaal first innings, Don Mackay-Coghill was hit in the groin by a ball from the 19-year-old Mike Procter and left the field. Batting at number five, Lance was propping up an end while wickets fell around him. At nine down, Mackay-Coghill made his way gingerly back to the wicket with Tony Tillim as a runner. Transvaal were 204 for 9, with Lance on 55 not out.

Although in huge pain, Mackay-Coghill and Lance started putting together a solid partnership and moved past numerous milestones: they avoided the follow-on; Lance scored a century; they made a 100-run partnership in just over an hour; they took the record for best last-wicket stand for Transvaal (breaking the record of 104); and finally the pair broke the South African tenth-wicket partnership record of 129, which had stood for 40 years.

When the two batsmen were just eight runs short of overtaking Natal's first-innings score, which would have given them vital bonus points, they took a suicidal second run and Lance was run out for 168. He and Mackay-Coghill (58) had put on 174 runs for the tenth wicket and the match eventually ended in a draw.

Lance stormed into the Transvaal dressing room, threw down his bat and swore about the umpires. His teammates asked him if he had been unfairly given out. 'Oh, I was out all right!' said Lance. 'But did he have to put up his finger so quickly?'

What a difference an over makes

A Currie Cup match between Eastern Province and Rhodesia in Bulawayo in November 1972 ended in uproar when Eastern Province captain Lorrie Wilmot took his side off the field, believing that the game was over and his side had salvaged a draw. The rules dictated that 20 overs had to be bowled in the last hour of play. An over began just before a final drinks session was taken, 61 minutes before stumps were drawn.

An Eastern Province player asked umpire Chris Sweeting if this was the first of the 20 overs. Sweeting was hesitant in his answer, saying: 'I'm not sure, I think so.' During the drinks break, the umpires then made it clear that the previous over had not been the first of the allotted 20 overs and they instructed the third umpire to tell the media and the scorers.

Wilmot wasn't happy with the decision, and after the 19th over had been bowled, he led his side off the field, saying the game was over. It was delicately poised, with Rhodesia needing only six runs to win outright, and gain ten invaluable bonus points, which would have put them in a very good position to win the Currie Cup for the first time in their history.

Only the umpires and the two not-out batsmen, Rhodesia's captain Mike Procter and Paddy Clift, stayed on the field. The Eastern Province players, insistent that 20 overs had been bowled, had gathered just beyond the boundary. Umpire Sweeting called play loudly so that the Eastern Province players could hear him. They made no effort to come back onto the field. Procter was getting agitated and said if they didn't come back, he could claim the game. Sweeting called play two more times before lifting the bails and awarding the game to Rhodesia.

Although the umpires had acted in accordance with the laws, the South African Cricket Association investigated the matter and eventually ruled that the match had ended in a draw. Rhodesia appealed, but to no avail. The result caused such uproar in Rhodesia that there was talk of the country refusing to play in the Currie Cup. Given that there was nowhere else for the Rhodesians to play cricket, this was very much an empty threat. With Rhodesia just five points adrift of joint log leaders, Transvaal, Eastern Province and Western Province, the failure to get ten points for a win robbed them of a Currie Cup title, which Procter later described as a bitter pill to swallow.

Knocking some sense into him

South Africa's World Cup match against the United Arab Emirates in Rawalpindi on 16 February 1996 was marked by two extraordinary events. Batting first, South Africa knocked up 321 for 2 in their 50 overs, with opener Gary Kirsten scoring a mammoth 188 at better than a run a ball. He hit 13 fours and four sixes off 159 balls at a strike rate of 118.2.

The second extraordinary incident was the stupidity of UAE's captain Sultan Zarawani, who came out to bat in a floppy, broad-brimmed sun hat instead of a helmet. As he took strike, Pat Symcox baited fast bowler Allan Donald, who was waiting to bowl to Zarawani. 'Knock some sense into him,' urged Symcox. Donald promptly hit Zarawani on the head. His hat flew off as he fell to the ground. Donald admits having had a few worrying moments, as he thought he might have killed Zarawani. However, Zarawani managed to bat on, and when he was out seven balls later for a duck, he was taken to hospital for a check-up. South Africa won the match by 169 runs.

Slow off the mark

South Africa, Transvaal and Lions spin bowler Clive Eksteen was never a nervous batsman. That's why he was quite content to bat for over an hour in a Test match without getting off the mark, to set a South African Test record.

In the Centenary Test at Eden Park in Auckland in March 1995, Eksteen came to the wicket in the unusual position of number five batsman as a nightwatchman. He and Daryll Cullinan saw out the remaining few overs to the close, with Cullinan on 82 not out and Eksteen on 0 not out. As nightwatchman, all he had to do was make sure he didn't lose his wicket. Runs weren't important.

The next day, he continued to thwart the Kiwi attack before finally getting his first run after 64 minutes at the wicket. And then he went into a comparative batting frenzy, scoring 21 runs in the next hour before losing his wicket. He had batted for two hours and three minutes, facing 92 balls. South Africa won the match by 93 runs.

Eksteen was never the fastest run-scorer in Test matches. In his seven Tests, he scored 91 runs and faced 571 balls. That translates into a strike rate of 15.9, which means he scored at less than a run an over.

To be fair to Eksteen, he never had the job of chasing runs. He was invaluable in holding up an end, and helped three teammates to their debut Test centuries. When Jonty Rhodes got 101 not out against Sri Lanka in Moratuwa in August 1993, Eksteen got four in 92 minutes off 89 balls to force a famous draw. Similarly, Eksteen was at the other end when Brian McMillan got his first Test ton of 113 against Pakistan at the Wanderers in January 1995, with Eksteen getting only 13 in just over two hours. And he supported Dave Richardson to his debut Test century of 109 against New Zealand in January 1995 in Cape Town. Eksteen got his highest Test score that day – 22 in just under three hours.

The longest time taken to get off the mark in a Test match is 97 minutes by England's wicketkeeper Godfrey Evans against Australia in Adelaide in January 1947.

The longest duck in South African cricket was 'scored' by Zimbabwe/Rhodesia's Vince Hogg. Playing in a Currie Cup match against Natal B in Pietermaritzburg in January 1980, Hogg got a duck in his side's second innings after being at the wicket for 87 minutes. Amazingly, he and Ed Parker put on 64 runs for the tenth wicket, with Parker (and extras) doing all the run-scoring work.

South Africa was involved in the longest duck in Test cricket when New Zealand's tail-ender Geoff Allott took 101 minutes and 77 balls to get a duck in the first Test against South Africa in Auckland in March 1999.

The talented Mr Crisp

Bob Crisp was one of the most colourful cricketers South Africa has yet produced. Crisp's legacy to South Africa might be as founder-editor of *Drum* magazine in the 1950s, the magazine that became the quintessential black publication (before having a fall-out with the publisher Jim Bailey over content). But Crisp was so much more that the list of his achievements is long and exhausting.

Crisp has a number of dubious cricketing claims to fame. He holds the record for the most Test ducks in a row. He made four ducks in five balls in the third and fourth Tests against Australia in Cape Town and Durban in January and February 1936. The fourth Test was the last he would play for South Africa.

Twice in his career he took four wickets in four balls. Playing for Western Province against Griqualand West at the Old Wanderers in Johannesburg in a Currie Cup match in December 1931, Crisp took 8 for 31. Over three years later, he repeated the remarkable four wickets in four balls for Western Province against Natal at Kingsmead in March 1934, taking 9 for 64. He also took four wickets in five balls for Western Province against Transvaal at the Old Wanderers in January 1932, but his hat-trick was separated by a wicketless ball.

His nine wickets for 64 in that Durban game was enough for the selectors to include him in their victorious tour of England in 1935, where he took 107 wickets. He had been told he was in the team shortly after climbing Africa's highest mountain, Kilimanjaro – a feat he achieved twice in a fortnight. His best Test figures were 5 for 99 in the drawn fourth Test at Old Trafford, taking 13 Test wickets in the series at a shade under 20 runs an over.

Born in Calcutta and raised in Rhodesia, Crisp's journalistic career began on the *Bulawayo Chronicle*. On one occasion, as a cub reporter, he was sent by his news editor to cover an athletics meeting. He handed in his report, with the news that one RJ Crisp had won three of the main events. The news editor was naturally incredulous, asking Crisp if he was trying to be funny. 'Not at all,'

Crisp insisted, explaining that when he had arrived at the athletics meeting he discovered that there were still a few places available in some of the races and so he had entered himself and just happened to end up winning them all.

He served in the third Royal Tank Regiment in World War II in Greece and North Africa, about which he wrote two books, *The Gods Were Neutral* and *Brazen Chariots*. As a tank commander, Crisp was brave to the point of recklessness, losing six tanks. But he never shirked from fighting and was decorated for his bravery, although he was something of a 'turbulent' character who rubbed his superiors up the wrong way.

He was awarded the Distinguished Service Order for his gallantry, but behind the scenes he had apparently been anonymously feeding a Labour Member of Parliament information on the shortcomings of the tanks the British were using. The Labour MP used the information to ask Winston Churchill difficult questions in parliament.

He wasn't perhaps as anonymous as he thought, for Field Marshal Bernard Montgomery himself may have got to hear of his trouble-making and he intervened personally when his commanders recommended him for a bar with his DSO. Montgomery downgraded it to a Military Cross, despite Crisp's being mentioned in despatches no fewer than four times. Crisp won his MC for directing his armoured squadron during the Battle of El Alamein under heavy artillery and anti-tank fire. He was wounded twice in six weeks. After the Western Desert, he saw action in Greece and Normandy, from where he was eventually invalided back to England. An urban legend has it that he met the King once and was asked if the shrapnel in his head would affect his bowling. 'No, sire, I was hit in the head,' he apparently said. It may not be true, but the legend of the man continued to grow.

He was described as a 'serial womaniser and crooner in the nightclubs of Alexandria'. He worked as a journalist for several newspapers as well as *Wisden*, swam Loch Lomond, farmed minks in England and wrote leaders for the *East Anglian Daily Times*.

After some time sailing the Greek Islands, he was diagnosed with incurable cancer and moved to Crete, spending a year walking around the island, writing about his experiences for the *Sunday Express*. He beat the cancer, attributing his cure to copious bottles of red wine.

He died in March 1994 in England at the ripe old age of 83. Legend has it that a copy of *Sporting Life* was found in his lap and a stub for a £20 bet.

In a nine-year first-class career, Bob Crisp took 276 wickets at an average of 19.88; in nine Tests he took 20 wickets for 37.35 apiece.

A spread-out hat-trick

Jackie McGlew is the only bowler to have taken a first-class hat-trick, yet never to have taken three wickets in an innings. Playing for Natal against Transvaal in a Currie Cup match in Durban in February 1964, he took the wicket of Tony Tillim to wrap up Transvaal's first innings, and then with his first two balls in the second innings he got the wickets of Ian Fullerton and Gerald

Innes for an unusual hat-trick. His match analysis was 3 for 17 off 10.3 overs.

Team effort

South Africa can sometimes take this 'we play as a team' lark a bit far. They are the only team to have had all 11 players involved in all of the wickets taken in a Test innings – and they have done it twice.

They first completed this feat in 1999 when they beat England at the World Cup. In the second innings of the fifth Test against the West Indies in Kingston in 2000/01, every single member of the team was involved in taking the wickets of the West Indians in one way or another. They repeated this against England at Newlands in 2010.

Against the West Indies, Shaun Pollock took four wickets for 66 runs, but each of the bowlers chipped in with at least one stick. Allan Donald, Justin Kemp and Jacques Kallis took one each, while Paul Adams got two. Mark Boucher caught Leon Garrick for 27 off Donald; Pollock bowled Chris Gayle (32) and Marlon Samuels (59); Daryll Cullinan took a catch off Kemp to get rid of Shivnarine Chanderpaul (7); Adams bowled Brian Lara (14); Pollock took a catch from Carl Hooper (5) to give Kallis his wicket; Neil McKenzie snaffled high-scoring wicketkeeper Ridley Jacobs (85); Herschelle Gibbs and Cullinan gave Polly his third and fourth wickets with catches off Mervyn Dillon (13) and Dinanath Ramnarine (9); while

Gary Kirsten, the old man of the team, also got in on the act, taking a chance from Courtney Walsh (3) as Adams took the last wicket.

The West Indies scored 301 in their second innings. Batting second, South Africa struggled to 255 and lost the fifth Test by 130 runs, but won the series 2-1.

In the third Test against England at Newlands in 2010, an otherwise boring final day was suddenly brought to life as South Africa whittled through the England batsmen, but failed to grab the last and final wicket as Graeme Swann and Graham Onions held out for England to survive with the score on 296 for 9. It was the second time the two had batted to survive a late onslaught from South Africa in the series, having done so at SuperSport Park in the first Test.

Paul Harris took three wickets, having England captain Andrew Strauss caught by Hashim Amla, Anderson caught by Ashwell Prince and Stuart Broad by AB de Villiers. JP Duminy – brought on by Graeme Smith when South Africa were desperate in the hope that the youngster's 'golden arm' would start something – took two wickets, removing Paul Collingwood, caught by Kallis, and Matt Prior, caught by De Villiers. Dale Steyn also got a pair, although his spell of bowling to Collingwood must rate as one of the best displays of modern pace bowling in recent memory, and he deserved more. He bowled Jonathan Trott and trapped Kevin Pietersen leg before.

The rest of the six bowlers, except Kallis, who got none, took one wicket apiece. Morné Morkel had Ian Bell caught by Smith, and Friedel de Wet got Alastair Cook to edge one behind to Mark

Boucher.

At the World Cup in 1999, South Africa tore England apart, dismissing them for 103. Donald took four wickets; Kallis and Steve Elworthy snaffled two each; while Pollock and Lance Klusener weighed in with one apiece. Boucher, Gibbs, Cullinan, Jonty Rhodes, Hansie Cronje and Gary Kirsten were all safe hands and took catches.

It just takes three

South Africa were dismissed by a team using the least number of fielders involved in all 20 wickets in a Test match when they were beaten by England in Cape Town in 1889. Just three England players were needed to get rid of the South African batsmen twice. Johnny Briggs bowled 14 of them and trapped two others leg before; Arnold Fothergill bowled one and got an LBW; while Bobby Abel took a catch off him. *Wisden* reports there was also a run-out in the South African first innings, but no one knows who he was. Briggs had match figures of 16 for 28. England took a liking to South Africa, and on three other occasions – Port Elizabeth in 1896, Lord's in 1912 and Johannesburg in 1927 – only needed four players to knock South Africa over twice.

Biff's first ton

It took Graeme Smith an absolute age to score his first ODI century, and it wasn't until his 58th match against England in Port Elizabeth in February 2005 that it arrived. When it came, it came at the best of times for his struggling team.

South Africa could not buy an ODI win at the time. In their last 14 matches over the space of a year, South Africa had only managed to beat Bangladesh, were beaten 12 times and then drew against England at Bloemfontein three days before the game in Port Elizabeth. Smith did not play well, offering up chances to England, which gave him two lives thanks to some clumsy and uncertain fielding under the poor lights of St George's Park.

His 105 was the first century by a South African captain in an ODI, and as South Africa looked as though they might lose another match in the series, it was left to a former captain, Shaun Pollock, to steer them home to their second win in a year, victory coming by three wickets with five balls remaining. For Smith, it was a monkey off his back after he had been run out for 99 in South Africa's comprehensive 177-run win against Sri Lanka at SuperSport Park in November 2002. He became the first man run out for 99 in a one-day international as he tried to scramble the final run to mid-wicket.

It took Smith just two more games after Port Elizabeth before he scored his second ODI century in the fifth of the seven-match series against England in East London, scoring 115 not out in a seven-run victory for his side. South Africa wrapped up the series 4-1 at SuperSport Park with a solid three-wicket win.

In the family

Lonwabo Tsotsobe, the fast bowler plying his trade with the Warriors, made his debut for South Africa against Australia in the T20 match played at the Melbourne Cricket Ground in 2009.

He comes from a proud South African sporting family. His name had Shane Warne, doing a stint for the Channel 9 commentary team, in stitches as Mark 'Tubby' Taylor tied his tongue in several knots trying to pronounce it. Lonwabo's sister Nomsebenzi was the first captain of the women's Springbok rugby team, and has been listed as one of the 'beauties of sport' by a South African magazine for her looks as well as her sidestep.

Their father Toto played rugby at a representative level in the 1970s, while their mother organises women's rugby in the Port Elizabeth area, and their brother Langa turns out at wing for the Pirates Rugby Club in Greenside, Johannesburg.

X marks the spot

X marked the spot for Lundi Xhanti Xhongo when the Cape Town-born player represented Western Province in the UCB Provincial Cup in October 2004. He was the first player with the letter 'X' in his name to play a first-class match in cricket when he went onto the field against North West at Newlands. His first-class career didn't last too long. He didn't get to bat, as Province scored 276 in their first innings and declared. Then he wasn't needed to bowl in North West's first innings, as they collapsed all out for 98. He bowled seven overs for 11 runs in the second innings, with two maidens and no wickets as North West collapsed again for 98, and Province won by an innings and 80 runs. It was his only first-class game.

This one's on me

This comes without any official confirmation, but a quick survey around the press boxes and bars of the country reveals that Herschelle Gibbs is probably the most fined player in South African cricket history. It would take more than these pages to list all of Gibbs's infractions, but the man has had more than his fair share of trouble. After winning a man-of-the-match award at an ODI at Newlands, not long after he had been fined R25,000 by the team for staying out past curfew during the Test against England in 2005, Gibbs joked that the money for the award might go some of the way towards paying his fine.

Gibbs got into serious trouble in 2000 when he was banned from all cricket for six months for taking $25,000 from Hansie Cronje to be dismissed for a low score in a game. That Gibbs forgot about this arrangement was neither here nor there. He was in trouble again five months later after smoking dagga with four other players in the West Indies. He, Roger Telemachus, Paul Adams, André Nel, Justin Kemp – and physiotherapist Craig Smith – were fined R10,000 each.

In April 2000, he was in trouble with the then United Cricket Board when he was caught out at a nightclub in Cape Town in the wee hours before an ODI. Summoned to a disciplinary committee, Gibbs shocked the members of that body when he arrived without any legal representation and dressed casually. With three legal experts on the committee, Gibbs was asked if he wanted representation. 'Nah, you guys will be fair,' was his reply. The charge was read out to Gibbs, listing all the sections and subsections and including the phrase 'conduct unbecoming'. Gibbs was a little nonplussed and said he thought he was in trouble for being out at a nightclub. When he was banned for three games and fined R15,000, with the games and R10,000 of the fine suspended, Gibbs asked: 'Is that R10,000 like a deposit?' Indeed.

He stayed out the night before the fifth day of a Test against England in 2005, which South Africa were favourites to win, and was initially fined R50,000 by the team, which was later cut to R25,000, the maximum fine the team could impose.

After being dropped again in 2008 for being out late at night, Gibbs spent a month in a rehabilitation centre to help him with his drinking problem. From the look of things, it seems to have done him the power of good.

It's mine; no, yours ...

It took four people to effect Mondi Zondeki's first international wicket. Mark Boucher may have been as surprised as Zondeki by the fact that Marvan Atapattu got an edge to a delivery just wide of the off stump, which nipped away slightly. As Atapattu chased it, attempting to steer it through the slips, he edged it to Boucher, who fumbled the straightforward chance. Luckily, Andrew Hall was beside him at first slip and took the deflection with a fine one-handed catch.

TV times

At 1.53pm on 26 February 2009, the country that had introduced video technology to the world of cricket experienced the Umpire Decision Referral System, when it was used in South Africa for the first time in a Test match.

The International Cricket Council had, in its infinite wisdom, decided that one of the most important series in Test cricket in recent years – the winner of the three-match series would be crowned the number one Test team in the world – was the ideal occasion to try out the new system.

On the first day of the first Test at the Wanderers, Ricky Ponting was cut in half by a snorter of a delivery from Morné Morkel. The South Africans appealed, but were turned down. They asked the umpire to refer the decision to Asad Rauf, the television umpire, but replays showed that the delivery brushed Ponting's pocket.

South Africa were only successful once with the referral system; Australia had more success. Unsurprisingly, the South African captain Graeme Smith said he was not at all happy with the decision, whereas Ponting thought it was okay.

In truth, though, this was the first 'official' referral. Years before, Hansie Cronje had engineered the first actual referral request during the fifth and decisive Test between South Africa and England at Newlands in January 1996. Cronje was desperate for a victory after the first four Tests between the two countries had been tied and after Graham Thorpe, who had been playing well, slipped a Paul Adams delivery down leg and set off for a quick single. He was run out, but given not out by South African umpire Dave Orchard, who did not call for the third umpire. Cronje, alerted by the cries of dismay from the South Africans who were watching on television in the boxes around Newlands, implored – nay, demanded – that Orchard refer the decision upstairs. The ICC rules then stated that the umpire makes the decision when to call for the third umpire and should he decide not to, the fielding side dare not ask him to change his mind. Orchard did, and the third umpire found Thorpe was short. South Africa won the Test within three days and, therefore, the series. However, Cronje paid for his indiscretion and was fined 50% of his match fee (R6,000) by the referee Clive Lloyd.

Turn on the TV

On 14 November 1992, umpiring in cricket changed forever when television technology was used for the first time in a Test match. Sachin Tendulkar became the first man dismissed by TV replay, ruled run out from a Jonty Rhodes underarm throw. Karl

Liebenberg was the TV umpire, and Cyril Mitchley, standing at square leg, had referred it to him.

Ali Bacher had seen the future of cricket on a television at Heathrow Airport back in 1992. He was on his way back from an ICC meeting in July and as he waited for his flight to Johannesburg, caught some of the Benson & Hedges Cup Final in the departure lounge. It was Hampshire against Kent at Lord's, and, those being the days before Duckworth and Lewis, the limited-overs match, which had been curtailed because of rain, simply continued on the next day from where it had left off.

'I remember it so clearly,' said Bacher. 'Graham Cowdrey, the son of Colin, was batting for Kent. He took a quick run and David Gower, from backward square leg, hit the stumps with a direct throw. My immediate reaction was "not out". The umpire said the same thing, and Cowdrey was ruled in.'

Then came the moment of revelation. The BBC showed a replay: Cowdrey was out by a good metre. The naked eye had told a lie. The naked truth was very different from the perception. It was a lightbulb moment for Bacher, who mulled over the decision on the flight home. He'd just seen the future and it involved cameras and slow-motion replays. It made such sense.

'When I got home, I called Mike Demaine [SABC Television sports producer] and told him my idea,' said Bacher. 'We decided that two cameras either side of the wicket would be ideal for judging run-out and stumping decisions. It was a simple thing to do. The next thing was to convince the Indians, whom we were hosting later in the year, to go along with the plan. My board (the United Cricket Board) and the South Africans were all for it, but Mohammad Azharuddin, the Indian captain, and their team manager were a little wary of it. Clive Lloyd was the match referee for the series, so I asked him to have a chat with them. Let's just say he "leaned" on them a little.'

Four months after Bacher had watched Cowdrey survive a run-out, Tendulkar was run out – but there was still a sceptic. Steve Bucknor, the West Indian umpire, was the other umpire in the series and made plain his misgivings about the technology.

'He said straight up he didn't like it,' said Bacher. 'But in the next Test at the Wanderers, he gave Jonty Rhodes not out after an appeal by the Indians. Jonty was on 28 at the time and eventually scored 91. We had been in a lot of trouble in the first innings and Jonty's knock saved South Africa. Steve later saw the replay back at his hotel and he told me he was horrified when he saw Jonty should have been out. He had thought he was well in. To his great credit, he came to a press conference the next day and said the new system clearly worked. That was the key moment for using technology in sport.'

Like fathers, like sons

Michael Owen-Smith and Patrick Compton – the sons of Tuppy Owen-Smith and Denis Compton – are two prominent South African cricket journalists, who have travelled the globe covering South Africa, and whose fathers played international cricket.

Michael Owen-Smith was appointed the South African cricket

team's media liaison officer in 2007. His father Tuppy Owen-Smith, born Harold Geoffrey Owen, in Rondebosch, Cape Town, in 1909, played five Tests against England during the 1929 tour to England. He hit 252 in his short career, with a high score of 129 at Headingley, Leeds. He was also an Oxford blue in cricket, rugby and boxing, and played ten rugby Tests for England as a fullback, three of them as captain.

Denis Compton played 78 Tests for England, scoring almost 6,000 runs at an average of more than 50. He was famously absent-minded; in 1955, he once arrived to play South Africa at Old Trafford without his kit. Colin Cowdrey remembers that this didn't worry Compton in the slightest. He walked into the Old Trafford museum, took an antique bat from a display and scored 155 and 79 not out. He was also well known for running partners out. Trevor Bailey commented that a 'call for a run from Compton should be treated as no more than a basis for negotiation'. Compton also played on the wing for Arsenal when they won the FA Cup in 1950 and the league in 1948, and for England 12 times during the war.

Rudi boy

The 2007 Cricket World Cup final in the West Indies between Australia and Sri Lanka finished in the dark and caused much anger around the world, and a South African umpire, Rudi Koertzen, was among those blamed.

Sri Lanka and Australia were made to play out three overs in the dark because certain people didn't know the rules. Match referee, Jeff Crowe from New Zealand, who is well paid to sit inside a suite at the ground, watch the match on TV and then arbitrarily fine players to show he is necessary to the game, blamed the third umpire, Rudi Koertzen, for the mess: 'Rudi is a South African, so he has a larger voice,' said Crowe. Obviously, he thought that South Africans are louder and more expressive than the Kiwis.

Speedy Zondeki

Politician and activist Steve Tshwete was Mondi Zondeki's uncle and father figure, but the South African and Western Province fast bowler comes from one of the most prominent families in South African cricket.

Zondeki's great-grandfather Samuel formed the Zondeki Cricket Board in Izeli in 1939. Zondeki's mother was the sister of Steve Tshwete's wife and the young Zondeki lived with them from the age of seven, spending time in exile in Zambia. Tshwete never got to see his nephew bowl for South Africa, but Zondeki dedicated his first match to his uncle and got a wicket with his first ever ball in international cricket, having Marvan Atapattu caught in the slips in an ODI in Bloemfontein in 2002.

Zondeki attended Dale College in the Eastern Cape, the same school in which Makhaya Ntini was a rising star. Zondeki was initially a leg-spinner, but Greg Hayes, who had also identified

Ntini as a quick-bowling talent, suggested he take a bigger run-up and bowl faster. He did, and during a game against an England schools team at under-15 level, he forced four batsmen to retire after hitting them on the elbow.

JP Squared

There are only two Duminys to have played international cricket in the history of the game thus far, and not only are both of them from South Africa, but they also share the same initials, both are left-handed batsmen, both were born in Cape Town, and they are distant relatives – third cousins, thrice removed.

They also got their breaks in the South African team in the same way – through an injury to another player.

Jean-Paul Duminy, the current young star, had shown promise, but burst onto the scene in the 2008/09 season, having been taken to Australia as cover for the Test matches. The day before the first Test at the WACA ground in Perth, Ashwell Prince was smashed on the thumb by a quick delivery by Makhaya Ntini during a net session. His finger badly injured, Prince failed a fitness test the next morning, and Duminy was told he was to make his Test debut.

He didn't get off to the greatest of starts, bowled for just one run in the first innings, but he learnt his lesson and scored a determined 50 not out in the second innings as South Africa won the first Test.

Prince had not recovered by the Melbourne Test on Boxing

Day, and Duminy was kept in the team, which turned out to be a masterstroke. With South Africa in trouble at 251 for 8 and batting second at the MCG, Duminy and Dale Steyn took South Africa to 431 for 9 and by the time Duminy was bowled for 166, South Africa had taken a first-innings lead. They won the match and the series, and Duminy scored 246 runs at an average of 61.50.

In 1929, South Africa were touring England when they suffered a series of injuries that meant they needed a batsman desperately. They could not wait the time it would take to ship a player out from South Africa and so an emergency call was made to Jacobus Petrus Duminy, who was on holiday in Switzerland at the time. Dr JP Duminy played in the third Test of the series in Leeds and scored 2 and 12 in his innings as South Africa lost the match by five wickets. South Africa went on to lose the five-Test series 1-0. This was to be the last of the three Tests he played for South Africa.

According to Jon Gemmell's *The Politics of South African Cricket*, Dr Duminy was the first Afrikaner to play for South Africa. He was a Rhodes Scholar who attended Oxford University, and, according to *Wisden*, his talent was 'never truly reflected in his three Test appearances for South Africa. In two Tests against England in 1927/28 – opening the batting in three innings – he failed to reach double figures, and when called up as an emergency replacement while visiting Europe in 1929, he made only 2 and 12 in the Leeds Test, which was rendered memorable by the last-wicket stand of 103 in little more than an hour by "Tuppy" Owen-Smith and "Sandy" Bell.'

The 1920s Duminy displayed the same high level of fielding skills as his current namesake, taking a diving, one-handed catch in the gully to dismiss left-handed middle-order bat Maurice Leyland. Notes *Wisden*:

> Duminy made a strong impact on the game, scoring 95 not out in his first innings for Transvaal, against Stanyforth's 1927/28 MCC team at Pretoria, a week before his 30th birthday. A double of 55 and 74 not out in the return match earned him his Test place. Against Border in 1928/29 he made a big not-out century and took 6 for 40 with right-arm slows; but unspectacular performances in the other trial matches led to his omission from the tour of England – until he was tracked down in Switzerland! A Rhodes Scholar at Oxford in 1920, Professor Duminy – as he became – had a distinguished academic career, assuming the vice-chancellorship of the University of Cape Town, pursuing a courageous course in opposition to apartheid, and among other things, running cricket weeks for youngsters of all races.

Dr JP Duminy died at the Groote Schuur Hospital in Cape Town on 31 January 1980, aged 82.

Foreign stars

South Africans love to point out how many of their own countrymen were in the England team that toured South Africa in 2009/10, but of the more than 300 who have played Test cricket for South Africa, some 44 of them were born outside the borders of the Rainbow Nation.

The list includes:

- England (22): Harold Baumgartner; Richard Dumbrill; Charles Finlayson; Cyril Francois; Howard Francis; George Glover; Alfred Hall; Ernest 'Baberton' Halliwell; Frank Hearne; George Hearne; Philip Hutchinson; Percy Mansell; James 'Bonnor' Middleton; Charles Mills; William Milton; Frank Mitchell; Frank Nicholson; Dave Nourse; Tommy Routledge; Reggie Schwarz; George Thornton; Joseph Willoughby.
- Scotland: Tom Campbell.
- Ireland (2): Clement Johnson and Robert Poore.
- Rhodesia/Zimbabwe (9): Colin Bland; John du Preez; Steven Elworthy; Geoffrey Lawrence; Joseph Partridge; Anthony Pithey; David Pithey; Denis Tomlinson; Paul Harris.
- Mozambique: Dave Ironside.
- Swaziland: Lawrence 'Fish' Markham.
- India (4): Robert Stewart; Godfrey Cripps; Bob Crisp; Thomas Ward.
- Bermuda: Charles Hime.
- Java (Dutch East Indies): Frederick Cook.
- Egypt: John Traicos.
- Portugal: Richard Westcott.

Hey, what you doing this weekend?

George Parker was the first, and one must assume, the last man to represent South Africa at Test level without ever having played first-class cricket in South Africa. Born in Cape Town, Parker moved to England in 1920, but did not play a first-class game there either.

On the 1924 tour by South Africa to England, the captain Herbie Taylor found himself with a dilemma. In the ten matches before the first Test, Taylor's batsmen had been poor, but his bowlers had been shown to be spectacularly unsuited to English conditions, having beaten only Cambridge University. The team had drawn seven and lost two. Taylor decided to call up Parker, who had been playing for Eccleshill in the Bradford League, for a match against Oxford, their last warm-up game before the first Test. Along with Sid Pegler, whom Taylor had sent for after discovering his bowlers were poor, Parker took four wickets for 34 runs, and should have had more, had his teammates not grassed four catches. It was Parker's first first-class match.

Just 24 hours later, Taylor decided to put Parker straight into his team to play England at Edgbaston and gave him the new ball after England had won the toss and decided to bat first. His first spell as an international bowler was not pretty, according to the *Guardian*'s description: 'He is immensely deliberate as he walks to his bowling place; his eyes are cast on the earth, and he walks slowly and solemnly as though pondering mighty problems. The wildness of his bowling made a quite sensational contrast to his solid deportment.'

England took to him and thrashed him around the park, going to lunch on 122 without loss. However, refreshed and no doubt with a few words from Taylor in his ear, Parker bowled from the other end and bowled Herbert Sutcliffe for 64 with a superb yorker. England continued to make merry and after Dave Nourse, the left-arm medium-pacer, had damaged the webbing on his left hand while fielding, Parker was asked to bowl yet more overs, bowling for three hours on the trot. When Taylor relieved him, Parker walked off the field and into the team changing room, where Taylor found him slumped in a corner, exhausted. Thankfully, there were rest days in Test cricket then, and he had the Sunday off, but kicked off for South Africa again the following day, finishing with figures of 37-2-152-6 as England were bowled out for 438.

The South African batting, as mentioned, was not up to much, and South Africa were dismissed for just 30 runs in 13 overs and had to bat again. Parker was leg before to Arthur Gilligan for a golden duck in the first innings. Gilligan's figures were 6.3-4-7-6. Parker scored 2 not out in his second innings when South Africa scored 390, but South Africa lost by an innings and 18 runs.

Parker was kept in the team for the second Test at Lord's, but South Africa were not much better in that game. Again, they lost by an innings and 18 runs, but it was a horror show. South Africa won the toss and opted to bat first, scoring 273 – Parker's contribution being 1 not out. England had scored 28 at stumps, but the next day, Jack Hobbs (211) and Herbert Sutcliffe (122) led the charge as England scored more than 500, belting the South African attack to all parts of the ground. The *Wisden* report reads:

> Very seldom in a Test match has bowling been so mercilessly knocked about. In two hours and a half after lunch Hobbs and Sutcliffe added 200 runs, and in all, their partnership for the first wicket produced 268, this being a record in England for a Test match and only once surpassed – by Hobbs and Rhodes in 1912 in Australia. The running between the wickets was daring to the

point of audacity, but the two batsmen understood each other perfectly and never looked to be in danger. Sutcliffe was out first, at 268, pulling a ball from Parker onto his wicket.

Parker was the only South African to take wickets, getting Sutcliffe to play on and having Hobbs caught off a slower ball, to finish with figures of 2 for 121. He was bowled for a first-ball duck by Maurice Tate, the last man out for South Africa – his last action as an international player and his last first-class match. He was dropped for the third Test at Trent Bridge, which South Africa also lost, but only by nine wickets. They drew the fourth and fifth Tests, thanks to some rain, to end a wretched series of five matches: 'The tour in England was frankly a failure,' wrote *Wisden*.

Parker headed back north to play professionally in the Bradford League and later emigrated to Australia to play cricket. He died in Thredbo, New South Wales, on 1 May 1969, aged 69.

Turf wars

Part of the reason for South Africa's early failures when touring England was that they were used to playing their cricket on matting wickets, which are as they sound: heavily rolled ground with a mat of coconut fibre placed on top. Jack Siedle became the first South African to score the first Currie Cup and international century on a turf pitch.

The born and bred Durbanite hit 114 for Natal in December

1926 against Border in Durban. The Test century came in Cape Town in the 1930/31 season when he scored 141. He and Bruce Mitchell set a record of 260 for the first wicket against England. It was Siedle's only Test century.

His son John scored a century on his first-class debut for Western Province against Eastern Province in 1955/56, but had a short career in cricket, playing just five games for Province before ending his career with two matches for Natal.

A man of iron and nine and a half fingers

A man missing half a finger and just 51 days shy of his 50th birthday was responsible for South Africa being on the wrong end of the shortest Test match ever played, in terms of time spent on the field. In the 1931/32 season, Australia beat South Africa by an innings and 72 runs in a match at the Melbourne Cricket Ground which lasted just five hours and 53 minutes in total and was played on a horrifically sticky wicket. It was the lowest total by a team winning a Test match by an innings.

Bert Ironmonger, a slow left-arm Australian bowler and something of a joke with the bat, had lost half of his left forefinger when it got caught in a chaff-cutter on his family's farm. To slow the bleeding, Ironmonger's sister thrust his hand in a bag of flour. The injury did not hamper his future bowling career. Indeed, he could spin the ball prodigiously off the stump that was left behind on his left hand, as South Africa discovered at the MCG.

Aged 49 years and 314 days, Ironmonger, who had been the fourth oldest Test debutant at 45 years and 237 days, took five wickets for six runs in the first innings (7.2-5-6-5) as South Africa were dismissed for 36.

Australia scored 153 in their one and only innings before Ironmonger destroyed South Africa again, taking 6 for 18 (15.3-7-18-6).

After the match had started on a Friday, no play took place on Saturday and most of Sunday because of rain. On the Monday, however, it all happened, as proud Victorian Bill Lawry would say.

'In less than an hour and a half the last nine South African wickets went down for another 40 runs. Thus South Africa were twice dismissed for an aggregate of 81, the lowest total for two innings ever recorded in the history of Test match cricket. The wicket was very difficult and Ironmonger once more proved practically unplayable,' reported *Wisden.*

To make it worse, Australia managed to beat South Africa with just ten fit batsmen. Don Bradman did not play because, after South Africa won the toss and elected to bat, he managed to catch his studs on a rubber mat and twisted his ankle as he walked out to field. The injury was severe enough for him not to be able to play on the first day, but, as both captains had announced the teams already, Australia had to go into the first day of the Test with ten men.

Bradman was marked 'absent hurt' for the first innings as both South Africa and Australia were bowled out on the first day. He was fit to play after the rest day, but by then they had no need of the Don's batting.

Captains of the Caribbean

The first West Indian captain to play in the Currie Cup was not –
as one may assume – Alvin Kallicharran, but in fact Jackie Grant
of Trinidad, who turned out for Rhodesia in the 1931/32 season.
Kallicharran played in South Africa for Transvaal after coming to
the country as part of the controversial West Indies rebel side in
1983. Desmond Haynes was the overseas professional for Western
Province in the 1990s, and Brian Lara had a season at Northern
Transvaal.

One-ball Tich

Tich Smith got a remarkable pair in the Natal-Western Province
Currie Cup match in Durban in 1972/73. Facing just one ball
during the game, he was bowled first ball in the first innings and
then run out without facing a ball in the second.

Hand of Dey

Chris Dey, the Northerns wicketkeeper, was given out in a unique
way in the Currie Cup match against Free State in Bloemfontein
in 1973/74. He is the only non-striker to have been given out for
handling the ball in first-class cricket in South Africa.

One ball, big air

Trevor Quirk was better known for his cricket commentary, but he played 40 first-class games for Northern Transvaal as a right-hand bat and wicketkeeper. His bowling record in first-class cricket is the stuff of legends.

The only ball Quirk bowled in first-class cricket did not touch the ground. In a Currie Cup match between Northerns and Eastern Province in 1979/80, and with Eastern Province about to win, Quirk convinced his captain to let him take off the pads and have a bowl. The ball was a full toss, which Lorrie Wilmot promptly smashed for six to win the game.

Three first-class champions

Barry Richards, Kenny McEwan and Alvin Kallicharran have played for sides that won domestic first-class cricket competitions in three different countries. Richards for Natal, South Australia and Hampshire; Kallicharran for Warwickshire, Guyana and Transvaal; and McEwan for Western Province, Essex and Western Australia.

Stars from Stellies

Stellenbosch has provided many rugby Springboks down the years, but it wasn't until South Africa's first Test against the West

Indies that it was able to claim its first Test cricket players. Two Stellenbosch graduates, Peter Kirsten and Adrian Kuiper, played in the 1991/92 Test against the West Indies.

The Majola dynasty

The late Khaya Majola may be the most famous of all black cricketers. His name lives on in the Khaya Majola cricket week, a fitting tribute to one of the most important South African sporting families.

His father, Eric Majola, was the legendary 50s and 60s 'Bantu Springbok' in both rugby and cricket, and his brother is Gerald Majola who was appointed the CEO of Cricket South Africa in 2001.

Eric Khululekile Majola was born in 1930 and lived in the New Brighton township outside Port Elizabeth, where Khaya and Gerald were born in 1953 and 1959. The birth of his sons coincided with the heights of Eric's sporting career, when he represented the black Eastern Province and South African teams. He was a flyhalf and rated as being as good as Hansie Brewis and Keith Oxlee, and Cliff Morgan of Wales.

Although he didn't have his father's skill at rugby, Khaya was certainly a man blessed with considerable talent at cricket.

At the age of 19, with the South African government relaxing the rules about black and whites playing together following the D'Oliveira affair, Khaya was selected for a South African African

Cricket Board XI against a Derrick Robins XI in Soweto. Robbins was a wealthy man who attempted to break South Africa's sporting isolation. In 1974, Khaya was picked to play with Clive Rice in a Derrick Robins XI to tour England. Tich Smith and Rupert Hanley were among the others included in the team, but for Khaya the trip had more significance. Lennox Mlonzi, president of the South African African Cricket Board, declared Khaya would be the 'first African to officially play overseas'. He was correct, but, as André Odendaal wrote in *The Story of an African Game*, Nathaniel Umhalla and others had travelled abroad in the 1860s, albeit in a private capacity. None had represented the nation officially before – well, as official as was allowed in South Africa's fractious past.

Basil D'Oliveira was convinced that Khaya was talented enough to make it at the top level and felt that if he stayed in England for three seasons he would be a superstar. D'Oliveira also believed that had 'Eric Majola had my opportunities then you would have heard a lot more about him'.

Khaya returned with dreams of playing 'in a mixed Springbok side' one day, which he hoped 'wouldn't take too long'. Unfortunately, life in South Africa was not to be normal for some time.

Khaya captained the black Eastern Province side and when he was 35, the South African Council of Sport XI, but his belief in the unity of the Robins XI was 'a sham and … black players were merely being used as stooges to boost the chances of white South Africans playing international cricket again'.

He became involved in the South African Cricket Board of Control and fought for justice in sport and in life.

When South African cricket finally unified in the 1990s, Majola was the driving force behind transformation in the sport and development at grass-roots level.

Khaya Majola was diagnosed with cancer of the colon in 1998 and given just 12 months to live, but continued working until his death on 28 August 2000.

Gerald Majola became the CEO of the United Cricket Board on 1 January 2001, a job he was initially wary of taking. He had been approached by the UCB, but as a council member he was worried about a conflict of interest. He asked Nelson Mandela for advice and the great man told him to 'just go out there and do it for us'.

According to *Wisden*:

> Gerald Majola could play a bit too although records and statistics of non-white matches and careers during the apartheid years bear no comparison to the recognised 'first-class' structure. Simply organising and competing, on poor or artificial pitches, was achievement in itself and yet Majola's name features in every batting list there is: leading run-scorers [and] century partnerships. Among his favourite memories is the sixth-wicket stand of 145 he added with Khaya for Eastern Province against Transvaal in Johannesburg in 1986/87. Gerald made 117, his career best. He was a natural leader, too, captaining the South African Schools side to victory over the provincial B teams for a unique success in 1978/79.

The Majola family – a legend in South African cricket.

Jakes the lad

The fourth Test against the West Indies in 2010 was a game for South African records as Jacques Kallis confirmed his status as perhaps the greatest all-rounder the game has seen. Kallis reached 11,000 Test runs as he scored his 35th Test century and is the only player who has more than 10,000 runs and over 200 wickets.

What time's the start?

The Pietermaritzburg Oval is a venue rich in history and eccentricities, but has probably never hosted a stranger or more error-riddled match than the tour match between the West Indies and South Africa A during the 1998/99 season. The United Cricket Board, as it was then called, had allowed the provinces to keep the representatives of the South Africa A team for the Standard Bank League games the night before.

On the morning of the match, several of the South African players were still flying in to the game, so the UCB had to delay the start of the first day of the four-day match until they could be fetched from the airport. Missing from the team coached by Graham Ford were the captain Nic Pothas, Makhaya Ntini, Charl Willoughby, Shafiek Abrahams, Sven Koenig and Justin Kemp. Pothas finally took the toss at 1.30pm with Carl Hooper, the Windies captain, as Brian Lara had decided he needed a break after captaining a team that was getting hammered on the tour. They were 2-0 down in the Test series at that time, with three left to play. They eventually got beaten 5-0.

Dave Orchard and Wilf Diedericks were the umpires of the match, which was a typically dull tour game. The umpires decided to delay the start of the match because the run-up area for the bowlers from one end was damp. Just 34.2 overs of play had progressed when Orchard, without consulting a light meter, offered the West Indies, who were batting, the option of going off for bad light. They accepted it, much to the disgust of the decent-sized crowd of 3,000 who had arrived, and Orchard called play off for the day. Coming from Maritzburg, Orchard should have known better, though, because 30 minutes later, the sun was shining brightly and play was very possible – typical of Maritzburg, a place with four seasons in one day. The trouble was, Orchard had become ensconced at the little bar the umpires had, so the rest of the day was spent there, as a journalist who was drinking with them said, 'grogging properly'.

'I remember poor Wilf kept wanting to go back to their hotel, but Orchie wouldn't let him and Wilf ended up sleeping on a little couch they had in the bar.'

While Orchard was settling in, the South Africa A team had a football match while the Windies did some exercises. The Maritzburg Cricket Association President Mike Hickson fumed, accusing the UCB, the umpires and the batsmen of 'robbing the public'.

Five all out

Most South African cricketers marry once or, at a push, twice. Hugh Tayfield may have taken 170 Test wickets, five wickets in an innings 14 times and held several South African bowling records, but he also holds the record for being the most married Test cricketer. He was married five times, a record he holds with England batsman Bill Edrich from the 1940s.

Tayfield was known as Toey for his habit of stubbing his toes into the ground before every delivery, of which he bowled 13,568. And at the start of each over he would kiss the badge on his cap and then give it to the umpire.

One of his wives was an Australian, and the *Mercury* of Hobart felt that the story was important enough to run a picture of him with his bride on the front page of their Monday 24 May 1954 edition: 'Miss Barbara June Metcalf, of Perth (WA), with Springbok cricketer Hugh Tayfield after their marriage at the Emmanuel Cathedral in Durban. They met last year when Tayfield was touring Australia with the Springboks. The bride's parents are Mr and Mrs CF Metcalf, of Perth.'

The Fed from the East

One of the authors of this book is from the East Rand. (Hint: it is not David O'Sullivan.) He is a proud East Rander and takes every single chance he can to sing the praises of André Nel and remind everyone that Roger Federer is, in fact, not only half South African, but a South African whose mother is of East Rand stock.

And the Fed is a cricket fan – something he has revealed several times in his career. In 2005, Federer was watching the final match of the NatWest Series between England and Australia on TV before he was due to play Andy Roddick in the Wimbledon final. He went on to meet several of the Australian players and was apparently still talking to them five minutes before he strolled onto court and won in straight sets 6-2, 7-6, 6-4.

After the tsunami that caused such destruction in Asia in December 2004, Federer visited survivors in Sri Lanka in his role as a Unicef goodwill ambassador and played a pick-up game of cricket with children. He held a small wooden bat as kids bowled at him with a soft ball at a shelter camp in the Cuddalore district in the southern state of Tamil Nadu. Some 8,000 were killed there in the tsunami.

During a rain delay in a Masters Cup match against Lleyton Hewitt in Houston, Texas, in 2004 Federer played a quick game of cricket using a tennis ball.

In 2005, ahead of the Australian Open, he padded up for TV in a 'net' on the top of the Rod Laver Arena, and played a few strokes, impressing the Channel 7 commentators. 'Federer straight drove and cut the ball with such technique you would have been excused for thinking he had been playing the game all his life,' wrote *The Age* of Melbourne.

'I like playing cricket for enjoyment, but I don't think I could have made a living out of it,' Federer said in 2009.

André Gunther Nel

André Nel has an on-pitch alter ego called Gunther. He has this name because it is 'a good German name and sounds like someone who lives high up in the mountains so he doesn't have enough oxygen and that makes him crazy'.

Rocketman Robin

Robin Jackman is a kind man. Not only is he perhaps the best commentator on television in South Africa, but he knows how to be kind to very rich, very famous and very badly dressed pop stars.

Elton John, a huge cricket fan, arrived at Lord's to play in a charity cricket match and when he walked through the Long Room at the MCC he got horrid looks from the members: 'I had green hair and the looks I got as I walked through the Long Room … it was the longest walk out to the crease that I can ever remember and I thought "please let it end",' he said. 'I got to the crease and I thought "please let me score one run". I scored 24 but I got carried away. The next week, I played in Barnes and Robin Jackman got me out first ball.'

Jackers doesn't exactly remember bowling John first ball, but he does remember trying to teach him how to bowl leg spin.

Keep it down

South African television was kind of responsible for Australian team sponsors getting lots of free and extra media time during their tour of Bangladesh in 2005/06. Having just toured South Africa, the Australians found to their cost that the stump microphones were turned up a little higher than they were used to, and every one of their sledges during the second Test in Durban was being broadcast to an unhappy nation of South Africans and a grateful bunch of journalists.

Mike Hussey felt that the microphones were supposed to be switched off between deliveries, but the SABC did not do so. 'From a player point of view, the disappointing thing is that we weren't told they were on the whole time,' Hussey said. 'We were under the impression that they were only on for certain periods or they only broadcast certain bits that were said. So when we found out that they were basically doing the whole lot, then we were a bit disappointed.'

Tony Greig said that the sledging was some of the worst he had heard. 'I have never heard anything like it,' said Greig. 'I thought it might have something to do with the fact that we had a very, very good stump mike. We turned that stump mike up and we could hear every word out in the centre and it was unbelievable. It really was absolutely unbelievable. The Aussies love it.'

When they got to Bangladesh, the Australians made sure that if they had any comments, they would be ones that would make them money. So they began giving sponsors a plug: 'One for the boys at Travelex.' 'Plenty of energy from a Milo Energy Bar.' 'Phone home on 3 Mobile.' 'Keep it well oiled with Castrol, boys, come on.'

AB the voice

AB de Villiers, Gary Player and Benni McCarthy share something in common. The three have recorded songs and forced them on the public. De Villiers recorded an 'inspirational' song – 'Show Them Who You Are' – which can be downloaded from his website (www. abdevilliers.com). The lyrics include: 'Stand together, breathe as one, fight to win the game. It's time to be the best you can be.'

Over 40 years ago, Gary Player unleashed his recording of 'If There Was No You' to South Africans under the RCA label. The 'extended single' featured a picture of Player in a cardigan and white polo-neck shirt, and was given the title 'Gary Player Sings'. The other tracks were 'Treat Me Nice', 'Walk In The Sun' and 'Jenny'.

Benni McCarthy collaborated on a song with TKZee, a kwaito band, before the 1998 World Cup. It was called 'Shibobo' and, if we are to be honest, was a bigger hit than Bafana Bafana were at the World Cup.

Old Father Time

Sir Herbert Baker, the architect who designed the Union Buildings in Pretoria and many prominent buildings around Johannesburg and elsewhere in South Africa, designed the old Lord's grandstand, which was opened in 1926.

Sir Herbert presented Old Father Time, a steel weathervane in the shape of, well, Old Father Time to the MCC, and it sits on top of the Mound Stand. It has been there ever since, although it did once get knocked off by a cable attached to a balloon put up by the British Air Raid Precautions Service in 1940, which was to stop the Luftwaffe dive-bombing London.

Old Father Time at Lord's is a wizened old fella, who has 23.5-carat gold leaf on his scythe and on the ball beside the stumps. North, south, east and west are indicated beneath him. Cricket writer Lawrence Booth suggests that Old Father Time is only just older than the average MCC member.

You're not out, but you are

South African wicketkeeper Dave Richardson was once given out because the third umpire was either colour-blind or did not know whether green or red meant that the batsman was out. In the Wills Triangular Series match against Pakistan in Karachi in October 1994, the third umpire Atiq Khan was asked to rule on whether Richardson had been run out.

A few rewinds and slow-motion replays later showed that Richardson had made his ground, and Khan confidently pushed the green button to show that Richardson was safe. Unfortunately, the red light showed and the on-field umpires had no other choice than to rule him out for just seven runs. With the score on 137 for 7, the decision left South Africa in deep trouble. They were bowled out for 163 and eventually lost the game by eight wickets.

Jacket required

The year 1994 was a significant one for South Africans: democracy, freedom and the first tour by South Africa to England in 29 years. All of these things meant little to the stewards at Lord's, though. Archbishop Desmond Tutu, one of the greatest South African cricket fans, wanted to get into the South African dressing room at tea on the first day of the Test, but was stopped from doing so because, even though the stewards knew who he was, the Arch was not wearing a jacket and one may not enter the pavilion at Lord's if one is not wearing a jacket.

Following on in Mitchell's footsteps

Frank Mitchell played for South Africa and England, one of 14 people to do so, but the man who first represented England at the turn of the century and then so liked South Africa he did not leave, had a greater impact on cricket before his international debut in Johannesburg in February 1899.

Mitchell's actions as captain of Cambridge in a match against Oxford forced the authorities to make a change to the laws of the sport, making the follow-on optional from 1900. Before that, if a team had a deficit of 80 runs on the opposition score, the follow-on was compulsory. In what was termed 'unsportsmanlike behaviour', Mitchell decided he did not want Oxford to bat again and ordered his bowler, EB Shine (full name Eustace Beverley Shine, so he would probably want to be remembered as EB) to bowl the 12 extras required to make sure that the follow-on did not happen. The uproar was immediate and the condemnation – on the day from the spectators and the next day in the newspapers – was vitriolic. It did not help that three years before, Cambridge had done the same thing in a match against Oxford. In the 1893 match, Cambridge had scored 182 and Oxford were 95 for 9, and worked out that if they sacrificed their final wicket and batted again, then they had a chance of beating Cambridge on a crumbling wicket. The Cambridge captain, CM Wells (full names Cyril Mowbray, so we'll go with CM), ordered the bowler to bowl three wides on the trot, two of which went to the boundary.

The wound was still fresh in Oxford minds when Mitchell repeated the tactic in 1896. As *Wisden* wrote in their obituary of Mitchell: 'Members in the Pavilion stood up and shouted, "Play the game and play cricket". Frank Mitchell himself said that one irate gentleman threw a pair of field glasses at him. Such was the effect on the nerves of the Cambridge XI that they began their second innings most disastrously and, despite a recovery, they eventually suffered defeat by four wickets.'

Mitchell had some backers, though, in the venerated gentlemen at *Wisden*, who wrote: 'We defended FS Jackson and CM Wells for what they did and, believing that even in its amended form, Law 53 is ill adapted to modern cricket, we think Mitchell was quite entitled in the interests of his side to take the course he did. Opposite views were expressed during correspondence in the *Times*, but the authorities eventually changed the law so that the side batting first and leading by 150 runs should have the option of enforcing the follow-on or themselves going in a second time.'

Having not gone to a 'prominent school', as *Wisden* put it, Mitchell appeared from nowhere and began making runs aplenty for Cambridge. WG Grace marked him as one for the future; he featured for Yorkshire and was picked to tour South Africa with Lord Hawke's team in the 1898/99 season, a two-match series that England won 2-0.

Upon his return he was given a regular place in the Yorkshire XI, but returned to South Africa as a volunteer for the Boer War, fighting for the Yorkshire Dragoons. In his first-class career in England and playing for England, he scored 8,438 runs with an average of 32.45.

He was named one of *Wisden*'s Cricketers of the Year in 1902, but left later that year to return to Johannesburg. He worked as secretary to Sir Abe Bailey, the diamond tycoon, who had played three games for Transvaal, so it was natural that he should turn out for Transvaal. He captained them to Currie Cup success in 1902/03 and 1903/04, and captained the South African team that went to England in 1904. His second return to the land of his birth was not very auspicious. The triangular tournament of 1912, a brainchild of Bailey, was poorly attended and showed South African cricket at its weakest.

Mitchell also played rugby for England, earning six caps, and captained Oxford, touring America in 1895, 1897 and 1901. He wrote a chapter entitled 'Forward Play' for a book called *Rugby Football*, and also played football, keeping goal for Sussex.

Mitchell served in World War I, and also worked as a journalist. He died at his home in Blackheath, London, on 11 October 1936, aged 63 – a life lived to the full.

RIP Sir Aubrey, twice

Sir Aubrey Smith, the only Test player to have a star on the Hollywood Walk of Fame, may also be the first and only cricket player to read his own obituary in a newspaper. An issue of the *Graaff-Reinet Advertiser* in October 1889 published a notice in which Smith read that he had 'succumbed to that fell disease, inflammation of the lungs', which was a great pity, apparently: 'Much regret will be felt at his decease. He made many friends by his kindly disposition.'

He had, indeed, developed pneumonia, but survived and lived for 59 more years, so kind was Mother Nature to his kindly disposition.

His was a life well lived. Born in London, he was coached as a child by a famous Surrey player called Julius Caesar, captained England in the only Test he played, was a stockbroker and an actor who starred opposite Elizabeth Taylor and Greta Garbo. And a parody of the English character he portrayed appeared in an episode of the Simpsons.

Let's get the cricket bit out of the way first: a medium-fast bowler with a high action, Smith would approach the wicket in a curved run that earned him the nickname 'Round the corner', with *Wisden* suggesting that 'sometimes he started from a deep mid-off position, at others from behind the umpire'. WG Grace said it could be 'startling when he suddenly appears at the crease'.

He had a good first-class career for Sussex, taking 346 wickets at an average of 22.34 from 1882 to 1896, but only played one Test match, against South Africa in Port Elizabeth in March 1889. England won inside two days as Smith took 5 for 19 and match figures of 7 for 61. He captained England on that trip, their first tour of South Africa. It was Smith who was asked to hand over the cup donated by Sir Donald Currie, who founded the Castle Line shipping company, for the leading provinces to compete for.

He took a liking to the country and with Monty Bowden, a teammate who had played in two Tests on the tour, decided to move to Johannesburg to become a stockbroker. Bowden had taken over the captaincy of the England team for the second Test, which England also comfortably won.

Smith captained Transvaal during his time in Jo'burg, but later returned to London and took up acting for a living. His stage debut was as the villain Black Michael in the romance *The Prisoner of Zenda*.

He moved to the United States and into movies, where he played the quintessential Englishman. He was a character actor, acting the toff or the officer and, being so typically English, it was hard to miss him. He was six feet four with a handlebar moustache and bushy eyebrows. It is said that he would raise the Union Jack at his Mulholland Drive house every morning.

He gathered his countrymen around him and formed the Hollywood Cricket Club in 1932, levelling a field and building a pavilion at Griffith Park. He imported the grass seed from England, and regular matches would be played on the ground. He expected players to be available every week and once forced David Niven to attend a net practice. Niven was upset, as he had marked that night as one on which he was going to 'chase some skirt'.

Laurence Olivier, Boris Karloff and PG Wodehouse were just some who played on the field, although the club no longer exists, as the area was converted for the equestrian competition at the 1984 Olympic Games. *Wisden* wrote:

In 1937, during shooting of *The Prisoner of Zenda*, a boat carrying Gubby Allen's Ashes tourists docked for a few days and Smith was beside himself with joy, offering cinematic workshops to a bemused audience of Allen, Hedley Verity and CB Fry.

Another guest in Hollywood was Lancashire's Archie MacLaren, who arrived during the filming of *The Four Feathers*. MacLaren was hard up, as usual, and Smith paid his old crony some pin money as an extra. Many watchings of the film have revealed no sign of MacLaren's patrician features and the Lancashire captain may have been consigned to the cutting-room floor.

Smith was pompous and not over-endowed with humour but he can still be sent out with a good anecdote. During a game at Griffith Park he missed a sharp slip chance and his English butler was ordered to bring some spectacles, which he duly donned. With the next delivery the bowler produced an out-swinger and found the shoulder of the bat. This time the ball came into the slip cordon in a gentle parabola, offering the kind of catch that, as the old Robertson-Glasgow poem has it, 'a child would take at midnight with no moon'. Smith fluffed it and, as the ball fell to the turf, he snatched off the lenses. 'Damn fool brought my reading glasses.'

In a story that is probably apocryphal, it is said that on a trip to England Smith visited Lord's, where one of the members remarked: 'That man over there seems familiar.' 'Yes,' said the other. 'Chap called Smith. Used to play for Sussex.'

Smith did eventually die of pneumonia, but in Beverly Hills in 1948, aged 85, and not in South Africa.

The Burger boys

Jean de Villiers and Schalk Burger were once huge stars on the cricket field at Paarl Gym. The two put on 165 during a schoolboy match for their school, but it was Burger who had pretensions of playing the sport professionally once he left school.

When Burger left Paarl Gym he had a 'small cricket contract' in his pocket to play for Boland, but never got around to it because in his first year at Stellenbosch, he 'got a craving to play a bit of rugby, and Stellenbosch University picked me up in their system, and I told the cricket guys: "I am keen for a bit of rugby". The rest is history.'

Burger and his brother Tiaan played a lot of backyard cricket, which is easy when your backyard is your dad's wine farm and he has built you a cricket pitch to play on. 'That was our strength back then. We both ended up playing rugby but we've still got that pitch.'

The pitch is most definitely still there and at the family wine farm the Welbedacht Cricket Oval still exists and they also produce an award-winning wine called 'Cricket Pitch'.

The pitch at the oval was relaid a good few years ago, after the boys opted to follow their dad into rugby instead of cricket. One of the local clubs use the oval as their second ground and the farm hires the ground out to corporates for cricket days.

Burger was good enough to be one of 25 players to be selected by the United Cricket Board back in 2001 for an under-19 training camp at the Plascon Academy in Johannesburg. Among the others selected were Ryan McLaren, AB de Villiers, Hashim Amla, Russel

Symcox and a certain JP Duminy.

Victor Matfield was also a useful cricketer when at school, representing Far North.

Errol, the Currie Cup star

Because of the demands of modern sport, Errol Stewart will probably be the last ever man to win the Currie Cup in both rugby and cricket. The Currie Cup in cricket, of course, morphed into the Castle Cup and is now the SuperSport Series.

In 1995, Stewart became just the sixth player to win both rugby and cricket Currie Cups, and only the second to do so in the same year. He was a busy man in his playing days, was Stewart. He played centre for the Natal Sharks, kept wicket for Natal, was a lawyer by profession, did some television commentary work and was working towards getting a pilot's licence. So, he didn't have a lot of spare time.

He played in the same South African school team as Hansie Cronje and Jonty Rhodes in 1987 and then played for Natal for 16 years in 98 first-class matches, scoring 5,150 runs between 1988/89 and 2002/03 at an average of 38.78. He scored a double century, 11 centuries, 22 half-centuries and took 240 dismissals. He also played six ODIs for South Africa over the space of eight years, filling in when Dave Richardson or Mark Boucher were incapacitated.

He became involved in some controversy later in his career when he was picked by the United Cricket Board to lead a South Africa A team to Zimbabwe in January 2003, but refused to take up the offer on moral grounds. It was believed that his decision may have cost him a chance to be the back-up keeper to Boucher at the World Cup in March that year, but Stewart would not be budged:

> My conscience will not allow me to live in a luxury hotel in a country where people are dying of starvation. As someone in the legal profession, I am very sensitive about the abuse of human rights and the fact that the Zimbabwean judiciary is put under so much duress.
>
> I also don't agree at all with the way land is taken away from farmers. Ordinary Zimbabweans are being persecuted and there is no equal distribution of food in that country. Mugabe pays no heed whatsoever to democracy. There is starvation and I would never be able to forgive myself if I support a tyrant like Mugabe by going there to play cricket and give credibility to what he is doing to his people. I cannot think how any country could declare themselves willing to go and play there during the World Cup. They don't even have food for their own people. How are they going to provide quality healthcare in the event of a player or a supporter getting injured?

The UCB CEO Gerald Majola disapproved of Stewart's stance and there was a belief that it cost Stewart, then just 32, any chance of playing for South Africa at any level again.

Smith, the England captain killer

As one of the longest-serving captains on the international stage – only Ricky Ponting has been in the job longer – Graeme Smith has seen many captains come and go, but he seems to have developed a knack of forcing the resignations of England captains. On his first big tour as captain in 2003 (they had gone to Bangladesh shortly before), Smith went to England with a team still wounded somewhat from the fallout over the World Cup a few months earlier.

They showed little sign of that as Smith and Herschelle Gibbs turned Edgbaston into a scorched earth of a ground, putting on a partnership of 338 for 1, with Smith scoring a record 277 and Gibbs getting 179.

Nasser Hussain, the Test captain (he had resigned from the ODI captaincy after a poor World Cup), could find no answer to the South African batting, and as his team struggled, his mind was in turmoil. He scored just one run before being trapped leg before by Pollock, while a certain Michael Vaughan had banged 156. England survived the first Test, but Hussain didn't. He resigned after the Test, admitting that he didn't know what to do on the first day of the match: 'I wasn't quite the captain that England needed or wanted on Thursday.'

Matthew Engel, former editor of *Wisden*, wrote in the *Guardian* that it was 'the most surprising thing to happen in England since Harold Wilson walked out of Downing Street for no obvious reason 27 years ago'.

Derek Pringle, the former England bowler and now a celebrated cricket writer with the *Telegraph*, was a little less complimentary:

'He captained his country much as he led his working life, a human volcano constantly on the verge of an eruption. Walking away from the job he craved and had invested so much effort in was more painful than any of the broken bones he suffered in the line of duty.'

For Smith, it came as a surprise: 'I didn't expect it to happen, but Nasser obviously feels it is the best way forward for their side. I had been reading up on Hussain but now I suppose I'll have to read up on Vaughan again instead.'

Vaughan's first Test as captain against Smith wasn't a great start: South Africa thrashed them by an innings and 92 runs, Smith again getting a double hundred.

The series was eventually drawn, and Vaughan would travel to South Africa and get one over on Smith, but the South African would have the last laugh in the winter of 2008.

South Africa drew the first Test at Lord's, surviving after having to follow on. In the second, at Headingley, the cracks began appearing in Vaughan's demeanour. AB de Villiers claimed a catch off the England captain, but then immediately said he wasn't sure he had taken it, and South Africa suggested to the umpires that they get the third umpire to take a look. Replays showed he had grassed it.

Vaughan didn't take this well and in the team dining area he made a few biting comments about De Villiers in front of the media and players, suggesting he had cheated. Smith was nearby and gave Vaughan a piece of his mind. Game on.

In the South African innings Vaughan claimed he had caught Hashim Amla, a catch that looked as though it had touched the grass before he claimed it. Amla began to walk, as is his nature, but then stopped, as something felt wrong to him. South Africa asked for the catch to be referred and it looked to have bounced.

On the third morning of the Test, Vaughan was having a 'clear the air' chat with Mickey Arthur over the two catches, when Smith walked across and the two had a frank exchange of views. Smith said then he knew Vaughan was feeling the pressure and piled it on when South Africa won the Test.

When South Africa beat them by five wickets in the third Test and wrapped up the series, Vaughan fell on his sword. England could have won that third match, but Smith, just as he had done to Hussain, sucked the fight out of Vaughan with a match-winning innings of 154*. Vaughan resigned shortly after: 'The captain feels a little less pressure if he is performing well. There have been times when I have struggled and felt the pressure as a leader. To ask a lot of your players all the time when you're not performing well is a big thing.'

Kevin Pietersen has also come and gone, although that was entirely his own doing, and Andrew Strauss has also survived a tour against Smith. But there is still time ...

Hoggy's South African roots

Matthew Hoggard became one of England's top cricketers in the early part of the 21st century, but he has always said that he owed much of his success to the time he spent in South Africa at the end of the 20th century.

Indeed, Hoggard's early years were defined by South Africa. After playing a few seasons with the Yorkshire Second XI and making his first-class debut against South Africa A, he couldn't crack into the first team and the opportunity came to play for the Pirates club in Johannesburg.

Those who got to know Hoggy around that time will tell stories of big nights out and long drinking sessions down in the Pirates clubhouse. He stayed with Gauteng Cricket Board and Pirates stalwart Barry Skjoldhammer and his family during that time and still refers to them as his second family. At Pirates he played with a team that included several who had represented their countries and played for the then Transvaal. There was former New Zealand captain Ken Rutherford, as well as Steven Jack and Mark Rushmore, who had played for South Africa.

He said his favourite job while at Pirates was tending the bar in the club's hospitality suite at the Wanderers, from where he got to watch Mike Atherton's rearguard action to save a Test match.

While at Pirates he played alongside two talented Jo'burg schoolboys, both of whom eventually left the land of their birth to play for England and New Zealand respectively: Michael Lumb and Grant Elliott.

Hoggard was almost struck by lightning while in South Africa after another big night. He took up a dare by fellow Pirate Bruce Smith to swim across the Emmarentia Dam and while doing so, a bolt of lightning struck the dam, sending a shock through both of them. What also shocked them when they tried to get out of the dam were the police officers shining their torches around the dam banks, checking for hoboes.

'I did learn a lot more than how to live the high life in Jo'burg,' wrote Hoggard in his autobiography, *Hoggy*. 'My eyes were opened in a much broader sense by having to make friends in a foreign country, by learning the culture, working out what makes different people tick and how to fit in with them. The experience made me more capable of standing on my own two feet in the future.'

In August 1998, after he had finished his second stint at Pirates, he was asked to bowl in the nets at Headingley to the South Africans before the start of the one-day series against England and Sri Lanka. Bowling with a white ball, he was swinging and seaming prodigiously, and bowled out Hansie Cronje, Shaun Pollock, Jonty Rhodes and others. Corrie van Zyl, the South African bowling coach at the time and later the head coach of the Proteas, walked up to him and asked him if he had any plans for the winter. He accepted a contract to play for Free State and a few months later was back in South Africa.

Free State wickets are hard and flat, and Hoggard learnt patience as a bowler and was soon first choice in the team. His most important lessons as a bowler, though, came from Allan Donald, who worked on Hoggy's rhythm and showed him more than just a few tricks of the trade. This would come back to haunt South Africa later.

It was also while at Free State that Hoggard got to sign his first autograph as an England international – even though he wasn't yet an international. He was pulled over for speeding at 180km/h on a trip from Bloem to Cape Town. The police officer heard his accent, learnt that he was playing cricket and asked: 'Hey, you're not here playing for England, are you?'

'Yep, I sure am,' lied Hoggard.

'Oh, I don't think you need worry about that ticket, then. You can tear it up on one condition. You give me your autograph.'

Hoggard did so. Two months later, he made his Test debut.

He also learnt some Afrikaans during his time in South Africa, some of which he used on the cricket field. Once, while playing Eastern Province, he was frustrated by Louis Koen, who was hanging around for ages, getting ones and twos. Koen then got an inside edge for four off Hoggard, who reacted: 'You spawny f***ing c**t!'

Koen walked down the wicket, squared up to him and said: 'If you ever, ever call me that again, you little shit, I promise I will wrap this bat around your head.'

In Hoggard's next over, Koen did it again, another inside edge for four. Hoggard could not contain himself: 'You spawny f***ing *doos!*'

Koen looked up and started laughing. Ah, the beauty of Afrikaans in sport!

Hoggard returned to South Africa for the 2003 World Cup, but hardly played. On his next visit as a player he came out early and played for Pirates for a few months before England came to tour in 2004/05. Hoggard was fitter than ever, and when England went into the Wanderers Test with the series at 1-1 and two matches to play, he felt right at home.

He had played at the Bullring for Free State against Gauteng twice and both times had nightmare games, once going for 82 off 12 overs in a SuperSport Series match.

Nine years before he had watched Atherton and Jack Russell being heroes for England from a hospitality suite; now he had to work a little harder. He admitted he bowled like 'a pile of poo' in the first innings, 34 overs for 144 runs, but still picked up five wickets. In the second innings, though, 'something clicked'.

South Africa needed 325 to win on the last day, but England only had two sessions to bowl them out. It was all Hoggard needed.

In his third over, he trapped AB de Villiers (3) leg before; bowled Jacques Rudolph (2); had Jacques Kallis caught at slip by Marcus Trescothick for a golden duck; Boeta Dippenaar (14) was caught by Ashley Giles; Mark Boucher was caught by Simon Jones for a ten-ball duck; Nicky Boje (18) was caught and bowled and, with time running out, Dale Steyn (8) was caught by Simon Jones.

There were just 8.3 overs left in the day and Hoggard's innings figures of 7 for 61 were excellent, but his match figures of 12 for 205 were the best by an Englishman since Ian Botham 25 years before.

After the match as Barry Skjoldhammer, then Vice-President of the Gauteng Cricket Board, walked onto the field to congratulate him, Hoggard hugged him and said: 'Sorry, sorry, sorry, sorry, sorry.' It was an apology he didn't really mean, and he smiled as he gave it. But he hadn't broken every South African heart that day. In Pirates and Bloemfontein there were many who were proud at the small part they had played in his rise.

South African centuries on debut

How many South Africans have made Test centuries on debut seems a simple enough question. Kepler Wessels, Andrew Hudson and Jacques Rudolph are the obvious answers. However, that is to ignore those South African-born players who have represented other countries. There are three others: the Johannesburg-born Andrew Strauss scored 112 against New Zealand at Lord's in 2004; another Jo'burg lad, Matt Prior, scored 126 not out for England against the West Indies, also at Lord's, in 2007; and Cape Town-born Jonathan Trott scored 119 in England's second innings against Australia at the Oval in 2009.

South African England captains

Kevin Pietersen, Andrew Strauss, Tony Greig and Allan Lamb are all South Africans who have captained England, but Greig is the only one of the four who didn't score a century on his debut as the captain of the team. He came close though, getting 96 in England's first innings against Australia at Lord's in August 1975. It was the highest score in England's total of 315 before Greig was caught off the bowling of Max Walker by his now fellow Channel 9 commentator, Ian Chappell. The match was drawn and England eventually lost the Ashes 1-0.

Lamb scored 119 in England's first innings against the West Indies in Bridgetown, Barbados, in 1990. Again, it was the highest score, ended by Curtly Ambrose with a successful leg-before appeal. As England were batting second, they were on a hiding to nothing in Bridgetown as Ambrose took eight wickets in the second innings, in which four England players scored ducks, and the West Indies won by 164 runs. The West Indies won the series 2-1, with one match abandoned.

Pietersen has not been the most popular of South African-born captains, either in South Africa or in England, but his enforced resignation in 2009 after just three games was bizarre. Apparently Pietersen did not actually resign when he was in South Africa on holiday, but that's another story. Pietersen scored his debut ton as captain against South Africa in 2008, getting exactly 100 at the Oval before Jacques Kallis took a catch off Makhaya Ntini. England won the game, but South Africa had already wrapped up the series 2-1 for a historic win.

Strauss was born in Johannesburg, but left for England when he was still a child. He was named as a stand-in captain for Michael Vaughan at Lord's in 2006, and hit a composed 128 in the second innings against Pakistan. The match was drawn and England won the series 3-0, which included a controversial win in the match at the Oval when they were awarded the game because Pakistan had the sulks after being accused of tampering with the ball. At the time of writing, Strauss is the current captain of England.

Never bowled

Zimbabwe's Mark Dekker has the distinction of being one of the few batsmen never to be bowled throughout his career, although with an average of 15.85 from 14 Test matches, that might not be something he would care to bring up.

In 22 innings he was leg before seven times, caught 14 times and not out once. In the match in which he carried his bat, the second of a three-Test series against Pakistan in Pakistan in December 1998, the left-hander set a world first when he became the first batsman to bat through an entire innings without losing his wicket and not be the highest scorer. He scored 68 not out off 167 balls in 288 minutes, but was passed by the number three batsman, Alastair Campbell, whose 75 came at a sprightly pace, taking only 144 balls and 176 minutes. Dekker had also scored 68 in the first innings. Zimbabwe, unsurprisingly, lost the match.

The two-day Test

Two days Zimbabwean cricket will want to forget are 7 and 8 August 2005, when they lost a Test inside two days to New Zealand in Harare.

Their fast bowler, Christopher Bobby Mpofu, will want to forget 8 August more than the rest of his teammates, though. He became the first batsman to be stumped for a duck in both innings of a Test match in the same afternoon.

He must be a lover of symmetry, Mpofu, because not only did he go out for the same score in both innings, but was stumped by the same man – Brendon McCullum – and off the same bowler – Daniel Vettori – and after having faced the same number of balls – seven. Zimbabwe had been bowled out for 59 and 99 and lost by an innings and 294 runs.

Mpofu didn't help his team much in the second match, held in Bulawayo, when he wandered down the wicket to congratulate batting partner Blessing Mahwire on his half-century, and was run out for just three runs. At least Zimbabwe only lost by an innings and 46 runs in that match.

The match has echoes of the fourth Test between Australia and England in February 1895, when Bobby Peel was stumped for a pair at the Sydney Cricket Ground on the same day, the first player to have befallen this fate. England, who scored 65 and 72, lost by an innings and 147 runs.

Peel will probably be best remembered for being banned by Yorkshire after urinating on the pitch in 1897 during a game. That may not be entirely true, although Peel, rather worse for wear at the time, remembers being helped off the ground by the chairman of Yorkshire: 'Lord Hawke put his arm round me and helped me off the ground – and out of first-class cricket. What a gentleman!'

He bats, he bowls, he keeps

Tatenda Taibu, the diminutive former Zimbabwe captain and wicketkeeper, might have reached untold heights had he been born in another country. An exceptionally talented cricketer, the five-foot five-inch keeper showed his class in yet another losing performance for Zimbabwe when they played Sri Lanka in the second of two Tests in Bulawayo in 2004.

He did not give up a single bye in the Sri Lankan innings of 713 for 3 dec, a quite amazing feat of concentration and then the highest innings total without a bye being conceded. He kept to 993 balls, breaking the previous record of Hashan Tillakaratne, who was behind the stumps for a total of 671 for 4 (1,323 balls) against New Zealand in January 1991.

His record lasted five years and was broken by another Sri Lankan, Prasanna Jayawardene, who wore the pads as India scored 726 for 9 dec (981 balls) on a flat track in Mumbai in December 2009.

In the first Test of the 2004 series against Sri Lanka, Taibu, the captain of the team and desperate to break a first-wicket partnership between Marvan Atapattu and Sanath Jayasuriya that had already gone past 280, took off the gloves and bowled eight overs of off-break. He became the first wicketkeeper in history to bowl in a Test match and take the first wicket of the opposition. It was just his third delivery that fooled Jayasuriya, having him caught by Douglas Hondo for 157.

Taibu finished with figures of 1 for 27 from his eight overs.

Fletcher the engineer

Duncan Fletcher has had considerable success with Western Province and England, and now acts as a consultant to South Africa occasionally, but the Cape Town resident has had a varied and strange life.

The third of six children, Fletcher was born in Salisbury in Rhodesia on 27 September 1948. His sister Anne was the captain of the Zimbabwean hockey team that won gold at the 1980 Olympics in Moscow – a fairytale story, as the team was put together at the last minute after Zimbabwe was admitted to the Olympics following independence.

Fletcher was the first-team cricket captain at his school, but his early working days saw him as a systems engineer and one of his first jobs was to design his country's vehicle number-plate system. He described it thus to the *Observer*:

> The new format had to make it easier for witnesses of hit-and-run accidents to remember the number plate. So we added an alpha character to the end of the existing six-digit sequential system. The letters I, O and U were excluded, as they could be misidentified, leaving 23 letters to play with. The computer divided the six-digit number by 23. The 'remainder' would determine the letter; so a remainder of one would give you the letter 'A' on the number plate.

Such detail would help him later in his coaching career, but first he was picked to captain Zimbabwe in the 1983 World Cup, a team that included a 16-year-old Graeme Hick, later to play for England, as well as John Traicos, whose story is told elsewhere in this book.

Zimbabwe, an unknown factor, beat Pakistan in a warm-up match at the tournament, then shocked Australia, with Fletcher scoring 69 and taking 4 for 42 to be the man of the match. It was the biggest surprise of the World Cup then, and probably in the history of the tournament.

Fletcher moved to Cape Town and worked as a data-processing manager, but coached the University of Cape Town on the side for extra money. It was there that he encountered an 18-year-old Gary Kirsten. 'One day, Duncan sat me down and said, "Do you think you can play for Western Province?" And I said, "Hell, no." He said I could do it, but needed to get my arse in gear. To have someone backing you like that is so important,' said Kirsten.

Fletcher was appointed director of coaching at Western Province where he became a mentor to Jacques Kallis, teaching him how to switch off between balls.

Fletcher moved to England and coached at Glamorgan before he was appointed to the poisoned chalice of the England job in 1999, taking over from David Lloyd. His first tour was to South Africa and included the infamous SuperSport Park Test in which Hansie Cronje engineered a result at the behest of bookies.

In 2005, Fletcher led England to that famous Ashes win. He continues to live in Cape Town.

Marvellous Marvan, superb Sanath

After Marvan Atapattu and Sanath Jayasuriya had been dismissed for ducks in their first innings of the first Test on their 2000/01 tour of South Africa in the Boxing Day Test in Durban, it was left to a third-wicket partnership to not only give some semblance of respectability to the visitors' batting, but also to set a new record along the way.

With Sri Lanka chasing South Africa's first innings total of 420, Kumar Sangakkara (74) and Mahela Jayawardene (98), put on a third-wicket partnership of 168. The rest of the Sri Lankan batting collapsed with scores of 3, 6, 16, 2, 3, 5 and 0. The 9 extras South Africa gave away was the fourth biggest score in the total of 216.

Sangakkara and Jayawardene's partnership made up 77.78% of the total, the highest percentage in Test cricket. They surpassed the 76.54% totalled by Australia's Alec Bannerman (70) and Percy McDonnell (147), whose 190-run, fourth-wicket stand for Australia against England at the MCG in 1881/82 had stood for over a century.

Jayawardene gloved one off Lance Klusener to be dismissed and Sangakkara was caught by Gary Kirsten off Nicky Boje.

The Test match was also significant in that Shaun Pollock, at the age of 27, took his 200th wicket after Nuwan Zoysa attempted an extravagant pull and succeeded only in miscuing it to Mfuneko Ngam at mid-wicket.

South Africa were ripped apart by Muttiah Muralitharan in their second innings, collapsing to 140 all out. They were still favourites to win, but with the entire fourth day lost to weather, Sri Lanka saved the Test. Sangakkara and Jayawardene were heroes and record-breakers.

Sources

Barlow, E. *Eddie Barlow: The Autobiography*. Cape Town: Tafelberg Publishers, 2006.

Capostagno, A. *Memorable Moments in One-Day Cricket*. Johannesburg: Penguin Books, 2002.

Crowley, B. *Cricket's Exiles*. Cape Town: Don Nelson Publishers, 1983.

Dawson, M. *The Bumper Book of Cricket Useless Information*. London: Metro Publishing, 2009.

Griffiths, E. *Kepler: The Biography*. London: Pelham Books, 1994.

Hartman, R. *Ali: The Life of Ali Bacher*. Johannesburg: Penguin Books, 2004.

Kidson, H. *Over and Time: An Umpire's Autobiography*. Cape Town: Howard Timmins, 1983.

Knowles, R. *South Africa versus England: A Test Cricket History*. Cape Town: Sable Media, 1995.

Oborne, P. *Basil D'Oliveira*. London: Little, Brown, 2004.

Odendaal, A. *The Story of an African Game*. Cape Town: David Philip Publishers, 2003.

Pollock, P. and Pollock, G. *Bouncers and Boundaries*. Johannesburg: Sportsman Enterprises, 1969.

Pollock, P. *The Thirty Tests*. Cape Town: Don Nelson Publishers, 1978.

Procter, M. *Cricket Buccaneer*. Cape Town: Don Nelson Publishers, 1974.

Rice, J. *Curiosities of Cricket*. London: Pavilion Books, 1993.

Winch, J. *Cricket in Southern Africa: Two Hundred Years of Achievements and Records*. Johannesburg: Windsor Publishers, 1997.

Websites
www.cricinfo.com
www.cricketarchive.com